IRISH SHORES

A journey round the rim of Ireland

For Felicity

The true charm of pedestrianism does not lie in the walking, or in the scenery, but in the talking.

Mark Twain, A Tramp Abroad, 1880.

© PAUL CLEMENTS 1993

Published by Greystone Books Ltd, 1993
at Antrim, Northern Ireland

ISBN 1 870157 02 8
© *Illustrations by Barbara Allen, 1993*

Printed in Northern Ireland by W & G Baird Ltd

IRISH SHORES

A journey round the rim of Ireland

PAUL CLEMENTS

GREYSTONE BOOKS

ACKNOWLEDGEMENTS

Many people helped me with this book. Some read sections of the manuscript or all of it. Special thanks to James Hughes, who cast a critical eye over the first draft, Chris Murphy of Murphy's Wildlife, and my editor, Jane Crosbie, who has a fine feel for words. I am grateful for the information supplied by the offices of *Bord Fáilte* in each county along the route in the Republic, and to the Northern Ireland Tourist Board and district councils for the help and material they provided.

I would like to thank the following publishers for permission to quote extracts from their books: Faber and Faber Ltd. for permission to quote from the essay 'Through My Guidebooks' from *Travels* by Jan Morris, 1976, and Blackstaff Press for permission to quote from the poem 'Backside to the Wind' by Paul Durcan, published in the *Penguin Book of Contemporary Irish Poetry*, Penguin Books Ltd., 1990.

Most of all I wish to thank the people who picked me up along the way and gave me lifts in their cars and boats, and to those who guided me around and invited me into their homes; without them the journey recorded in this book would not have taken place. In some cases, names have been changed to conceal their identities.

Finally, I wish to make it clear that the opinions expressed are mine alone. They do not represent those of my employers, editor or publisher.

R. Paul Clements

1993

CONTENTS

Contents

INTRODUCTION

The idea had come to me at thirty-seven thousand feet up and at a speed of six hundred and three miles an hour. Over the last twenty years I had clocked up more than three hundred thousand miles of air travel and visited some fifty countries.

A shelf at home contained twenty photo albums. In them are memories of an African safari, Greek Island hopping, the Taj Mahal, the Kremlin, and New England in the fall. The peoples of the world feature from the covered market in Istanbul, servants on the houseboats of Kashmir, the floating market in Bangkok to the beach bures of the Fijian Islands. It is a collection housing more than three thousand pictures. All there as a testament to many gruelling hours spent cooped up in aeroplanes and to a commitment to seeing the world. The last holiday – a round-the-world flight – involved spending more than fifty-five hours on an aircraft, albeit spread over six weeks. It was this trip that finally led to what Americans call a 're-prioritisation' of my future holidays. I had come to my senses.

On the final leg of the circumnavigation of the globe I decided it was indeed a truly unsatisfactory method of travel. It was high time I saw my own country before it became submerged by the twenty-first century. Ireland, north and south, was out there waiting to be explored. Next time I would stay at home.

Over the years I had spent holidays in various parts of Ireland and was reasonably familiar with the contours of its mountains through hill walking and rambling expeditions. But there had never been enough time to linger in places and see what made the country tick. I wanted to let the people speak for themselves and I needed time to seek out the wild flowers and look at the birds.

When I arrived back on terra firma and returned home I found the idea of a trip around Ireland would not go away. It was like an itch. It niggled for sleepless nights and forced me to think about it in more detail. I wanted to become, in a sense, a part of the land through which I was travelling. I resolved to attempt to hitchhike around the coast, from Belfast, in a circle. The grand plan was to hug the coastline in an anticlockwise direction and avoid the cities, as far as that was practicable. I would head for the unsung towns and coastal villages, or at least wherever I was deposited at the end of each day.

Parts of the coast were unknown to me and I felt somewhat ashamed of that. I dug out Ordnance Survey maps of Ireland and settled down to some serious investigation. After a perusal I believed it might be possible, given sufficient luck and generosity by motorists, to complete the round trip in a month. I always had a hankering to take off and loved the idea of the open road. Over the years I'd hitchhiked on a small scale in the United States and Australia, as well as several European countries. These experiences had, for various reasons, been indelibly imprinted on my mind and I'd always managed to reach my destination – eventually.

In the days that followed my imagination became preoccupied with the scheme. Any spare time was taken up with more scrutiny of the maps. I spent long periods scanning the coastal route running my finger along the curves and pausing every so often to savour the names:

Easky, Caheracruttera, Blanket Nook, Pluck, Bedlam and Sneem leapt from the map; there were the islands of Adam and Eve; there was Bastardstown, Horetown and Heavenstown. What magical place names, and they'd been here all the time.

Although the Ordnance Survey maps of Ireland provided fascinating information they didn't tell me the nitty-gritty of what I wanted to know. Then I remembered about another large book on my shelves: The Atlas of Ireland. At first glance it seemed somewhat mundane in comparison with the World Atlas, but the details contained within its ninety-six pages were absorbing. There was everything from the number of households with toilets and telephones to the main areas of barley and wheat production, the distribution of population, urban morphology and demographic relationships. One page was given over to details of the mean monthly and annual rainfall at selected stations complete with wind speed and directions. A study of this revealed that either May or June were the driest months in Ireland, although this varied between regions.

As a prospective hitchhiker the map on page seventy-five grabbed my attention. It gave details of road traffic and the daily flow in vehicles. The figures were broken down into six categories and the frequency of vehicles was denoted by the thickness of a brown line. On the east coast near Belfast and Dublin the heavy line indicated a daily flow of more than twenty thousand vehicles a day. The lines, resembling a spider's web, spread out from the cities decreasing gradually at various stages throughout the country until they became, in some places – notably along the west coast – very faint, representing nought to one thousand vehicles a day. Here indeed was much food for thought. The sources at the foot of the page showed the information was gathered in traffic censuses more than twenty years ago, but most of it, I felt, would still be valid.

I'd come to the conclusion that because of the time limit on my odyssey I could not travel around every promontory or visit every isolated headland. To do so would take six months or longer. I would have to make a decision to skip some on the basis of progress made. Certainly if the traffic flow was less than nought vehicles a day then there wasn't much point in standing at the side of the road with my thumb in the air. With a ruler I carried out a rough calculation of the distances involved in a coastal loop. I worked it out to be about fifteen hundred miles, avoiding some of the peninsulas and headlands. A quick piece of arithmetic led me to deduce that over twenty-eight days I would need to cover an average of fifty-five miles a day – surely not an impossible goal.

There is one further factor which has not yet been mentioned. The small matter of my conjugal responsibilities and how the POSSLQ was going to react. Because of the complicated shift system which my work involves several days could elapse without seeing my wife, Felicity. For that reason she had become known to me, not in any offensive way, but in the form of a handy acronym as the POSSLQ (person of opposite sex sharing living quarters).

The subject of my heading off for a month had already been tentatively broached. It would not be the first time. I'd spent six months away from home working in London a couple of years ago. There had been re-unions most weekends but this was to be a full month away on my own. To make the project a success I felt I must have peace to think and write in my own time. I argued that it would be much more difficult for two people to hitchhike, and trotted out a couple of my favourite travel quotations: '*He travels fastest who travels alone,*' and one from Henry David Thoreau who said '*The man who goes alone can start today; but he who travels with another must wait till that other is ready.*' Naturally the thought of coming with me had never crossed her mind. The benefits of marrying an accommodating and understanding wife whose name means 'happiness' should never be underestimated. I would, of course, keep in touch on the telephone and write letters. In the event of an emergency or disaster I could be home within a day or so as I would not be leaving the shores of Ireland.

And so the dates were organized, the holiday leave arranged and the rucksack packed. Clothes, toiletries, camera and films, binoculars and notebooks were loaded in. I also brought the indispensable Ordnance Survey maps and area guides to each county along the route. Reading matter for the journey was most important and I packed a selection of books to help while away time spent at the roadside waiting for lifts. My *vade-mecums* included separate pocket guides to the wild flowers, birds, place names and mountains of Ireland, and a collection of contemporary Irish poetry. For some light relief I chose a book called *Greatly Exaggerated* containing the wit and wisdom of Mark Twain, and *The Adventures of Tom Sawyer*, on the basis that one should always have nearby a work by a Clemens, either with or without the T.

On this trip I would take great delight in leaving behind such items as fly spray, antiseptic cream, indigestion pills and antimalaria tablets. There was no need to worry about typhoid, cholera, polio, hepatitis, or tetanus injections. I could leave the air to the seagulls and airline companies, and not concern myself with jet-lag, strikes by airport controllers, immigration delays, airport taxes or lost luggage at the carousel. Visas, tickets, labels and suntan lotion I could forget about, and although I would be crossing and re-crossing a border, a passport was not required. Seen from this vantage, Ireland seemed an immensely attractive ground-level proposition.

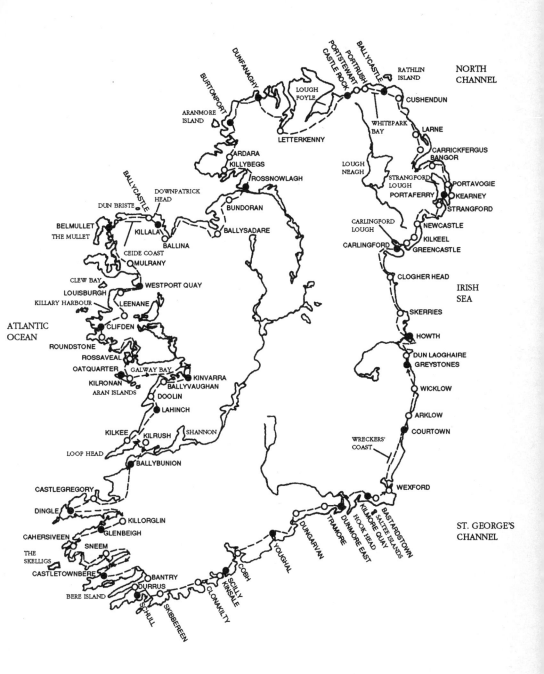

IN THE LAND OF UKOGBANI

Belfast to Ballycastle

The weather forecast for Friday the thirty-first of May is for another dry day with sunny spells. Winds will be light, temperatures will be around twenty, but it'll be a couple of degrees cooler on the coast. The outlook for the weekend is for mainly dry weather with more clear or sunny spells. I fervently hope the men at the Met Office will be casting their sunny spells throughout the month of June.

The day has now arrived. The day when months of dreaming turn into the harsh asphalt of reality. Felicity drops me off at a footpath near a roundabout on the Shore Road on the northern outskirts of Belfast. She is worried about my safety for the next four weeks. I promise not to accept lifts from drunken drivers or strange women. Roundabouts are not the best places for goodbyes, so after a swift farewell ceremony, I suddenly find myself on my own, standing at the side of the road with a heavy rucksack perched on my back, wondering what on earth I am doing.

Cars drive past me at speed. The road to Carrickfergus is a wide two-lane highway. When William Thackeray travelled this route for his Irish Sketchbook in 1842 he noted that the road *'was extremely lively and cars and omnibuses passed thickly peopled.'*

The road is still a busy one, but now a wide six-lane motorway brings traffic from Belfast. Not surprisingly most cars are going the opposite direction for me, heading into Belfast. Nevertheless I stick my thumb in the air and have a go at hitching a few vehicles. My appearance and demeanour is vitally important. I have opted for a casual mode of dress: a clean crisp T-shirt and a pair of lightweight trousers with large pockets for maps and guides. I want to look well groomed and tidy, but not overdressed. After ten minutes a red Cavalier pulls up and stops five yards in front of me. I run in eager anticipation to the passenger door and the driver shouts out to me.

'How far you goin'?'

'About fifteen hundred miles,' I reply, 'but Carrickfergus or anywhere in that direction will do fine.'

Greg Jones is the kind of driver the POSSLQ warned me to avoid. He takes great delight in recounting the number of spills and accidents he's had. He seems almost proud of the fact that he has been prosecuted six times by the police for dangerous and careless driving.

'In the last accident I damaged nine ribs,' he laughs. 'I went straight through the windscreen. Ended up with six broken ribs, and three cracked ones. I got glass in my hands, split some veins and suffered whiplash and bruises down the side of the head.'

Greg points to his temples and the side of his face. He smiles. I shift uncomfortably in my seat, and fumble to try to get my seatbelt on.

'Don't bother with those things, they don't work anyway,' he says. He gives me more information on his spills. 'I've been fined four times. Last was the highest though. A hundred pounds for dangerous driving.'

We drive through a section of the borough of Newtownabbey, past large detached houses which front on to the sea, and a new industrial estate in a former factory which Greg says was owned by Courtaulds.

He drops me along Marine Highway near the centre. I get out, slightly shaken, but glad to be back on the tarmac. It's nine forty-five. I've been on the road less than an hour, but feel in desperate need of a coffee.

* * * * *

The borough council is trying to do its bit in Carrick's economic recovery. In the tourist literature selling the town to visitors or possible investors from overseas it provides a gushing description:

> *Steeped in a wealth of historical legend, Carrickfergus is an unparalleled blend of the old and the new. Excellent restaurants, hotels, pubs, shops and a host of recreational facilities combine uniquely with ancient tradition to ensure an interesting and enjoyable visit, all within walking distance of the marina.*

The town is trying hard to live up to its motto: '*Gloria Prisca Novatur,*' The Glory of Old Made New. Over the centuries it has had many variants on its name as far as the spelling is concerned. For example: Cracfergus, Karefgus, Crafferg, Carifargus, Karikfarius.

The current spelling – Carrickfergus – is derived from the Rock of Fergus identified with Fergus Mor Mac Eirc, founder of the Dalriadan dynasty in north-east Ireland and south-west Scotland believed drowned at this rock around AD 530.

Along Marine Highway the cynosure is unquestionably the Castle. I'd visited the grounds before but had never been inside so I pick it as the perfect starting point to explore the past and give the journey an early boost with a look at the country from an historical perspective. I had not planned on a holiday visiting castles and museums, but this one is an exception.

In answer to a query about information the man in the shop at the entrance says there is a leaflet for ten pence or a book for six pounds. 'Now, how many books do you want?' he asks.

The castle was built as a stronghold in 1178 by John de Courcy after his invasion of Ulster. It was sited on the edge of a basalt rock with commanding views over Belfast Lough and the surrounding countryside. De Courcy later took Downpatrick and ruled Ulster for twenty-seven years. He picked Carrick as his capital because it was ideally placed for communication and supply by the sea.

The castle was taken by King John after a siege in 1210 and fell to the Scots in 1316. During the sixteenth century it was attacked several times. Then in 1760 the French, under commander Thurot, captured it. It was heavily defended during that siege by a group of young recruits. Half a dozen life-size models of these recruits now stand at one side of the castle ready for action. The models are a recent addition to the castle. They include Simon the Sentry, standing guard at the castle's back door; Godfrey the Gatekeeper, watching the entrance; Adam the Archer with his longbow looking out from the Keep; Faithful Fortescue washing the barrel of his seventeenth century cannon; Gilbert the Master Gunner, and the burly figure of Ronald of Richmond who was the constable of the castle in the fourteenth century and looked after the running of it when his lord was away. He controlled everyone from knights to door keepers, watchmen and messengers. He is depicted in a small enclosure dealing with a case against men trading with the Scots which led to fifty pounds' worth of seized goods being granted to him as a reward – a worthwhile return to a man who was normally paid forty pounds a year.

Surveying the scene is a large fibreglass statue of a Norman figure on the roof of the Keep with the de Courcy flag. He has become known to Carrick people, and to passing motorists who glimpse him from the highway as 'Stormin' Norman' (after General Norman Schwarzkopf, the allied commander of the Second Gulf War in 1991). I wonder what this particular Norman would make of modern technological warfare with its Scud missiles and jet fighters.

Today, besides the presence of the full-time custodian and the models, the only other occupants of the castle are a family of gargling black guillemots. They've made their home in a gap between stones in the wall at the seaward tip and are determined to stake a firm territorial claim to their right to be there. Overhead, starlings and hooded crows flit across the black-brown basalt stone wall. They seem to prefer the creamy yellow Cultra stone which the Anglo-Norman builders brought across the lough. A group of small rock pipits with their peculiar little squeak dive and bob around the grass.

Inside the Keep a variety of displays on three floors takes the visitor through the history of the castle and area. A wall chart covering the period from 1797 to 1843 features a copy of Pigot's Directory of 1824 which shows details of the people who lived in Carrick. I notice the postmistress was Elizabeth Clements whose job was to sort out the mail from Dublin and Belfast which arrived daily at twelve. Her other duties included sorting the letters for Larne, Glenarm and Cushendall which were to be sent out on the arrival of the Dublin mail. I also come across the name of one Ellis Henry Clements Esq., and find that he was listed among the gentry living in the town. I wonder where our family have fallen from grace. For my part, having been unable to find honest work after leaving school, I entered journalism and the rest, as they say, is literary history.

I squeeze down the spiral stairs. Bright sunshine lights up the gleaming Whiteabbey sandstone and eight hundred and thirteen years of history. John de Courcy, depicted on horseback, guards the original entrance to the castle. He looks every bit the glamorous hero and adventurous soldier: fair haired, blue-eyed, young and strong with his distinctive livery – red spread eagles on a white background. His saddles were made specially to support him so he could fight with both hands; it's said he fought more like a private soldier than a commander, lopping off the heads and arms of the natives with the stroke of his sword which was always at the ready.

A few yards from him sits his wife, the Lady Affreca. She was the daughter of the Norse King Godred of the Isle of Man. She sits on a window ledge of the Great Hall of the earliest castle against the east curtain wall, a somewhat unhappy looking figure. There was little natural light in those days so window seats were important for writing, sewing or simply day-dreaming and '*thinking of home.*'

The custodian, Ronnie Reid, who denies any ancestral link with Ronald of Richmond the fourteenth century constable of the castle, asks if I enjoyed my tour. I feel guilty as I have never before visited the castle but often drove past it. He tells me a story about a man who lived in Carrick for almost seventy years before he paid the castle a visit. The man had passed it twice a day on his way to and from work and he actually thought there was nothing behind the outside walls. It was only when American friends staying with him suggested they should go for a look round the building that he first saw inside.

Ronnie also tells me about another visitor – a man from Essex, who said he was touring UKOGBANI. I give Ronnie a puzzled look. He explains, with a wide grin, that the man was travelling through every district council area in the United Kingdom of Great Britain and Northern Ireland. Another acronym for my growing collection. I take my leave of Ronnie and of the castle in good humour having found something of the past come alive.

Outside, the waters of the North Channel are shimmering in the May sunshine. Three hundred yards from the castle, Carrickfergus marina is a much younger tourist draw and cannot claim the pedigree of its powerful neighbour. It was founded in 1985 and is called the friendly marina. The stylish brochure proclaims the management are committed to excellence. The information is willingly imparted by Errol Murphy, the customer services manager, who is keen to sell berths to anyone interested.

Much of the vocabulary of sailing contained in the brochure is a foreign language to me, not being well versed in nautical matters and brought up in the land-locked statelet of County Tyrone. The sub-culture of the sea has always been something of a mystery. In his small office Errol says there are boats in the marina valued from five hundred pounds up to two hundred and eighty-seven thousand pounds.

'There may be a recession, but it doesn't seem to affect the people who buy yachts and boats,' he says.

Carrick marina is vying for competition with Bangor marina across Belfast Lough. Errol feels Carrick is superior because it gets more sun. 'The sun shines for longer here than it does in County Down,' he claims.

'It rises there, comes across here, and sits over the Knockagh monument, so therefore it's here much longer.'

Before leaving the marina office I check the weather report for the day pinned to the notice board. It says visibility will be moderate or good and the weather will be fair.

I walk the half mile to the village of Eden on the other side of Carrick. On my left is an estate named the Garden of Eden with half a dozen modern houses. Unlike its biblical equivalent you would be hard pushed to describe it as a paradise. There are no signs of any apple trees nor for that matter naked women. But lest I be tempted by any hidden sin, I move along the main street and call in to Neill's shop where I eat of the forbidden fruit by purchasing a large east Antrim granny smith, served, I'm pleased to report by a fully clothed woman.

Within twenty minutes I get a lift to Larne with Gary Nelson in a Mini

1000. Gary is an apprentice bricklayer who comes from Larne. He is studying the building trade at technical college and wants to become a builder and eventually a teacher. He says it takes four years practical experience on site before he is able to enter the teaching profession. He takes me through Glenoe on the way to Larne. Along a straight narrow stretch we pass over a number of bumps on the road which Gary says are locally known as the 'Seven Sisters.'

* * * * *

When the travel writer, Paul Theroux, visited Larne in 1982 on his circumambulation of the coast for his book *The Kingdom by the Sea* he described the town as '*foreign-seeming, dark and gripping.*' It has every right to feel dark and despairing now. A few weeks before my visit the town (population 18,224) lost five hundred jobs with the announcement of the closure of a heavy engineering factory which had been one of the main employers in the area since the 1950s. For many of the workers made redundant – the fitters, welders and machinists – their best hope of work is represented in the sea. The ferries which cross to Scotland each day could take them to employment. Larne is the terminus of a short sea crossing from Britain. From Stranraer or Cairnryan, in Scotland, it takes just over two hours to cross the North Channel to the County Antrim coast.

From Larne I'm quickly dropped off at Ballygally. Over a sandwich and coffee in the bar of the Ballygally Hotel I watch the television news which carries a story about many parts of Ireland experiencing their driest May in a century. It was a month dominated by high pressure areas over the north-east Atlantic. Western Scotland had its driest May since records began. All this, I believe, bodes well for June.

I reckon I can be in Cushendun within half an hour if I get a decent lift. On this section of coast the traffic is not as thick as the road leading to Larne. Several cars with families pass me. Along the shore front two ringed plovers pick their way through seaweed looking for sand hoppers for their lunch. The sun is strong with a clear blue sky. It's the ideal day for hitching. On the telegraph wires a pied wagtail with its long black and white tail, makes a '*chizzit, chizzit*' call from its song-post. A black-headed gull searches for food, and a pair of eider ducks bob over the gentle waves.

The scenery along the Antrim coast road is justly famous. It starts as a corniche, and all along it's never more than a few yards from the sea. It has been called one of the finest scenic routes in Europe. Sixty years ago H. V. Morton, in his book *In Search of Ireland* (1930), wrote that he did not know eighty miles of road anywhere in the British Isles which can show more varied or entrancing beauty than this.

A lift with a retired couple takes me the seven miles to Glenarm where I'm picked up by Sammy Thompson who's work-dodging, though not from his employer. He's trying to postpone the awful moment when he has to wallpaper a bedroom in his house. He told himself that as it was so warm it was wrong to stay inside applying paste to bits of paper.

Sammy is on a day off from his work at Larne railway station and is going to Cushendall. He says he is looking forward to a hot summer, the way they used to be in the forties and fifties. The dialect takes on a whole new flavour here with a strong Scottish influence.

'We're owed a good summer this year,' he says. 'We had a very bad winter. It was freezin' cold in these parts for months and a very cold spring, and you usually find that fornenst that you get a good summer.'

As far as the local economy is concerned Sammy says the closure of the engineering works in Larne is a serious blow. 'Britain's buggered. You can't get a job round here. There's naithin' here for anybody.'

On the way Sammy points out some of the distinctive farms of the Glens area. They have a ladder pattern with fields of steep sides and dry stone walls. The coast and glens have been designated an area of outstanding natural beauty by the Department of the Environment which gives formal recognition to the quality of the landscape and the countryside of the Antrim plateau. Sammy says it's expensive to maintain some sections of the road because of landslips. Mud and rocks are constantly falling on the road during seastorms or floods. At Carnlough a sign proclaims it as a conservation area. From here the bay opens into a sweep round to Garron Point.

When I get to Cushendun, Sammy says I should look into McBride's pub, which is the smallest bar in the British Isles. I had read somewhere that it was the smallest in Northern Ireland.

From Cushendall it's a five mile hop over to Cushendun with a man who works in an hotel in the town. He doesn't tell me which one but he says if I'm spending some time in the village I should go to McBride's which is the smallest bar in Ireland.

Cushendun is preserved by the National Trust for its Cornish style whitewashed cottages with their slate hung roofs. The houses are neat and simple. The village name means '*at the foot of the Dun River.*' I check out McBride's Bar to get a measure of the place for myself. Ten people inside would fill it. At four-thirty this afternoon though there is no problem finding breathing space and elbow room – it is empty. When the barman eventually appears he assures me it is a well known establishment.

'This,' he proudly boasts, 'is the smallest bar in Europe.'

From Cushendun I'm faced with the first major decision of the journey. I want to try to get to Ballycastle and possibly stay there the night. I'd like to go via the coastal route, which takes in Torr Head, rather than the inland road, but resolve that my dilemma will be settled by whichever way I get a lift.

On the way out past hedges of escallonia I come to a junction where the roads diverge. As I've plenty of time to get to Ballycastle I try the coastal scenic route first. A robin red breast can't make up its mind where to settle and jumps from signpost to signpost. In a field in front of me a flock of sheep are asleep. Over the next hour fifteen cars pass. Only one stops and the driver offers to take me as far as Torr Head. This isn't suitable for me as I don't want to be stranded on the remote headland for the night. I walk across to try the inland road.

Another half hour passes at this peaceful roadside. I've now become engrossed in Tom Sawyer's adventures. At the start of the novel Mark Twain sets the scene by writing about the funny exploits Tom gets into. He says although the book is meant for the entertainment of boys and girls he hopes it will not be shunned by men and women. Part of his plan was to try to pleasantly remind adults of what they once were themselves, and of how they felt and thought and talked, and what queer enterprises they sometimes engaged in. I'd forgotten how superb a writer Mark Twain was. For the purposes of future references to him along this journey, I shall hereinafter refer to him as 'Uncle Mark.' In the meantime though I need to make some headway with my own particular 'queer enterprise' which is to try to hitch a lift to Ballycastle.

The woman running a caravan site behind me asks where I'm going. She says one of the men staying on the site for the weekend will soon be driving to Ballycastle and can give me a lift. In a few minutes a man called Harry McCambridge pulls out of the park and stops beside me. His wife gives up the front passenger seat and jumps into the back of the car with their three children.

My arrival in Ballycastle twenty minutes later coincides with the sun going down. A mist is settling in casting a shroud over Rathlin Island and enclosing the town. I check my rucksack into a small hotel in the centre and investigate one of the town's twelve pubs. According to the Northern Ireland Tourist Board brochure you can meet deep-sea fishermen, geologists, archaeologists, botanists, fossil-hunters, artists and amateur historians in Ballycastle's pubs. One of the hostelries, The House of McDonnell, is a building listed for its historic interest.

The young man behind the bar, Padraig Hill, says the previous night a group of twelve Lutheran ministers from Germany was in the pub. They'd been to Corrymeela, the peace community outside the town. He shows me the visitors' book in which they were asked for their comments and I'm amused at their views on the north Antrim landscape:

There are two much sheap's in your countrieside for our likings.
This meant they probably weren't indulging in the eight year old pure malt Scotch whisky behind the bar: The Original Oldbury Sheep Dip.

As I reflect on my first seventy miles on the road I look back on a moderately successful day of hitching; a quiet glow of satisfaction spreads over me, and I drink my first toast to the coast.

FOILED BY THE FOYLE

Ballycastle to Dunfanaghy

Ballycastle, on the Margy River, is a residential town. Its population of three thousand eight hundred is swollen during the summer with visitors coming to the caravan parks and campsites. People also travel from here to work in Coleraine, Ballymena and even Belfast, a distance of some one hundred and twenty miles return each day. Many of Ballycastle's business premises still have their original late Georgian shop fronts and the town is a conservation area. The historic core around the Diamond gives the place the harmonious appearance of a cosy traditional Irish country town. Over the years the owners of shops and houses have certainly taken care in the maintenance and upkeep of their properties.

I wander through the town to allow the traffic to build up and the temperature to warm up as it's a cold morning. The town is renowned as the site of probably the oldest fair in Ireland (the Oul Lammas Fair) which has been held on the last Monday and Tuesday in August for nearly four hundred years. As a journalist I've been sent to cover the fair on several occasions with the chilling parting words from the producer: 'Please try to get a new angle on the Lammas Fair and don't concentrate on eating the dulse or yellow man.'

On the road to Ballintoy hawthorn is growing in profusion in hedges along one side. A local farmer picks me up and says he is going just a couple of miles. From my vantage point on what is now the Causeway coast there are views across to Rathlin Island, while behind me the top of the gently curved Knocklayd Mountain is just about visible through a misty screen. The man who'd dropped me off said local people call it 'pudding mountain' because of its shape. It means the 'hill of breadth,' or broad hill.

11

The Causeway coast, which begins a few miles back at the north-east corner of Ireland, runs forty miles to Magilligan Point. Sandwiched in between are numerous towns and seaside resorts with large beaches. My aim is to get as far along it today as I can. My first view of the Atlantic Ocean shows it to be in a rough, turbulent mood, throwing off a biting wind. The day is a total contrast to yesterday. I had thought it might warm up, but if anything it is becoming colder and traffic is scarce.

A few farmers on tractors pass back and forth several times and give me a wave. In a field behind me bog cotton trembles in the wind. I would like a warmer coat. I've brought only a light windproof jacket. My teeth start to chatter, and my fingers and toes are beginning to grow numb with the cold. I'd love to keep my hands firmly planted in my pockets, but need to use my thumbs every so often and keep some circulation in them. The tops of them are turning into rosy hues with the cold. This being the month of June I had not thought of bringing gloves.

Inside the next half hour I count the number of cars that pass me on both hands, including thumbs. The eleventh one stops. It's driven by a woman whose baby daughter is strapped into the back seat. As we make our slow meandering descent into Ballintoy I begin to thaw out. I'd never realized the heater in a Peugeot 205 could exude so much warmth and even if it is only for a few minutes, it acts as a life-saver. When I tell her what I'm doing she gives me a bemused look which slowly turns to disbelief with a few shakes of the head. She wishes me good luck and drops me at the edge of the village.

A few fields, with a mixture of fat sheep and cattle, separate me from the ocean. A number seventy-two Ulsterbus sweeps past with several smug looking passengers. I study the map and pace up and down the road to try to generate some heat. The wind is unrelenting. A booklet on the area shows that a coastal path leads along to the Giant's Causeway. The route is peppered with little ports, meaning landing places, such as Portmoon, Port-na-Spaniagh, Portnaboe and Portnahooagh. A girl comes and stands near me. She thinks I'm waiting for the next bus, but when I tell her I'm hitchhiking she gives me a startled look and moves back into the village to wait in a shop. Forty minutes of standing around in the freezing conditions are rewarded with a lift from Ian, who describes himself as an amateur historian and archaeologist. He's going only as far as Whitepark Bay but for me anything is better than standing here.

Ian is on his way to the beach to take photographs of clumps of stones. He says he hadn't realized it was so cold. When we get there the only sign of life is two young boys who are trying to make a kite fly. On the beach below us about a dozen cows and bulls paddle along the front and wallow in the mud. It's a sight I've never seen before and the animals look extremely uncomfortable and cold. From the warmth of Ian's car I drink in the panorama.

He gives me a brief flavour of the history of the area. Whitepark Bay, he says, used to be a big industrial site during the Irish stone age. In those times the neolithic people lived on the seashore, but over the years their sites were destroyed by people who plundered them and thought there might be something valuable underneath them. The people lived on an exotic diet: lobster, shellfish, crab, flatfish and salmon.

Ian points to a small group of stones lying in the grass near the beach underneath which was a passage grave. There was also a dolmen on the hill behind and they were designed so that light from the setting sun shone up the passageway and lit up the chamber at the far end.

He says a huge community lived here with a highly developed culture. The stone age people set up a type of parish. They spent their time making and exporting stone axes, some of which were found as far away as northern France. The flint from the basalt cliffs was exported in shiploads throughout the British Isles.

The whole north Antrim coast is extremely rich in archaeological sites. These comprise passage graves or souterrains, standing stones, ring forts, dolmens, motte mounds, and the remains of churches, friaries, round towers and castles. Ian says practically every small peak in the area has a passage grave under it.

'Many old forts are hidden under gorse bushes and outcrops, and the ancient roads south of the coastal area have defensive mounds in fields,' he says. 'It was from these mottes the Irish defended themselves against the Normans. There really is so much to see here. You have to remember that this coast produced some of the earliest evidence for man living in Ireland. The point is that most people drive past these places at sixty miles an hour in their cars and don't know of their existence.'

I tell him this is the reason why I am hitchhiking and why I have left my car at home. I want to learn something of the country's past and meet people along the way. I thought I'd absorbed enough history for the morning and must now make progress. In three hours I've covered a mere ten miles. I make my way back on to the neolithic bypass in search of a lift. I watch several layers of Atlantic rollers come to a frothy end at the beach, which stretches from Portbradden with the smallest church in Ireland, or for all I know possibly all of Europe, over to Elephant Rock at the eastern end.

It was from the youth hostel at Whitepark Bay that a young Australian once hitched what turned out to be the longest ever recorded lift in a vehicle. He was picked up by four Americans in a Combi van. They took him through Ireland, Scotland, Wales, England, France, Andorra and into

Spain. It was estimated they covered nearly four and a half thousand miles together before separating. At the end of all that time spent together the Aussie must have been on extremely friendly terms with the people who took him on board.

I'll be content to settle for something a little less ambitious. Anywhere further along the north coast will do nicely. Never mind the delights of mainland Britain or Continental Europe the lights of Portrush or Portstewart will adequately fit my bill.

Fifteen minutes elapse. Several cars with families and English registered vehicles pass. None has room for me anyway, even if they stopped. Then the break that all hitchhikers need comes my way in the form of two Dublin girls in a Honda Civic. They're spending the weekend touring the north coast and are heading for Bushmills and Portrush with the intention of stopping to look around Dunluce Castle. I climb gratefully into the back seat. Lorraine and Susan say their plans are flexible and they don't have a fixed schedule.

Dunluce Castle stands on an isolated rocky promontory hanging on to the edge of the cliffs. It was built around 1300 as the stronghold of the MacDonnells, the chiefs of Antrim. An information sign says that during a storm in 1639 the kitchen crashed into the sea with most of the cooks, except for a tinker who was sitting in a window area mending pots.

We climb over some walls on to the steep slopes which lead down to the sea and search for wild flowers. On one bank there are masses of sea thrift or pink, known as 'daisy of the Irish seashore.' Some further searching reveals sea campion with its narrow leaves. It is a plant of the seaside and rocky coasts and is a subspecies of bladder campion. The word campion is said to be derived from the use of the flower as a wreath for the champions at the public games in the middle ages. Here too we find kidney vetch, a rich yellow-flowering perennial.

Below us a group of unsteady canoeists is trying to come to terms with the freezing water, but it doesn't worry a pair of eider ducks who turn over several times and spring up again. As I look out to sea I think about what Ian had told me earlier about the richness of north Antrim in terms of monuments and ancient sites.

Lorraine and Susan are enthralled by the approach to Portrush. Even on a dull day the combination of beach, sea and sand dunes makes it a spectacular view. They drop me in the centre of town and go off in search of food, promising to pick me up later if they see me on the road to Portstewart.

I mooch around the town and get the impression that Portrush, despite the crowds of people, seems to wear an air of despondency. The place looks in need of a complete lick of paint. The plasterwork and architectural details are fading on many buildings and at one end of the town there is a huge gap where the Northern Counties Hotel once stood. The building was burnt down in a fire in 1990 and, over a year later, nothing has been done to fill the hole. Part of one wall is visible with the doors and windows open to public view. In all, it represents a sorry sight.

At the other end of town the neo-Tudor railway station, which is a listed building, has been turned into a nightclub called 'TRAKS.' The train, with its connections to Belfast, is regarded by many as a major part of Portrush's problems bringing with it what a man in a local coffee shop describes as 'riff-raff from the back streets of Belfast.'

The town mostly caters for the money spinning day trippers or week-long family visitors in the summer. Tacky amusement centres with their bleeping electronic games, fast food stores and a host of souvenir and gift shops selling trinkets and hats line the main street. The hats are adorned with messages such as 'Kiss me slowly, squeeze me tight,' 'It's not easy being a sex symbol' and 'Sex Instructor: First lesson free.' For some inexplicable reason a collection of trays with pictures of the sea front of Bridlington are in the windows of several gift shops. The town has a small tourist office which on this Saturday afternoon in June is shut.

Undoubtedly the place is in need of a little imagination to spruce it up. In fact it looks in need of an overhaul to improve the shabbiness of the buildings. A team of decorators and landscape gardeners could work wonders. Portrush is also full of the twin evils of lager louts and litter. The latter caused in most cases by the former. The streets are covered with empty beer cans, crisp bags, fast-food wrappings, and ice-cream papers. Women, looking tired and beleaguered, push prams along the pavements while their husbands sit in pubs and hotel lounges passing the afternoon with friends.

I come to the conclusion the town doesn't need to worry about its image. It gets the visitors anyway but to me it seems to get the visitors it deserves. I walk on to the Ballyreagh Road looking for a lift to Portstewart. My luck is in. Within a few minutes the Dublin girls return again to pick me up. It appears I have established a personalized coastal taxi service with them. They aren't impressed with Portrush either and say it's not the place for them.

Over the years Portrush and Portstewart have virtually coalesced yet there remains a world of difference between the two. Three miles separate them but most of that is eaten up with caravan parks and camping sites, restaurants and pubs, holiday flats and apartments, and residential hous-ing. It is all mostly spread along one side of the road while the sea beats the cliffs on the other side. The lift takes me over the county border into Londonderry. I take my leave from the girls as I don't want to overdo my exploitation of their petrol tank.

Portstewart developed in the early part of the nineteenth century and the first houses were a few fishermen's huts built in the 1790s. Two hundred years on the resort has spread out to its present population of ten thousand. Many live in the new estates built around the edge. The town has a general air of freshness which its neighbour is lacking.

The beating heart of Portstewart is the promenade. It is made up of three and four storey buildings overlooking the Atlantic and the hills of Donegal across the water. The front has a mixture of shops, supermarkets, pubs, guest houses and a bank or two. There are several small hotels and the now obligatory residential home which occupies a corner site in a former hotel. This is one growth industry and a fact of life as the population continues to live longer. Portstewart has traditionally been a retirement home for people and the town takes pride in its gentle pursuits. The tourist board leaflet says there are tennis, bowling, putting greens and bracing walks for the more active.

I have a fairly warm attachment stretching back to childhood holidays with the place. Carrick-Dhu, Juniper Hill, Dhu Varren, The Strand and Morelli's Cafe are names redolent with summer holidays in August. For personal reasons I have also frequented it in recent years as the DOIM (dear old Irish mother) has retired here.

Before leaving I make a brief pilgrimage to Morelli's. The ice-cream cafe smack in the centre of the prom has been a fixture of life here for several generations. A large sign outside announces their eightieth birthday, from 1911 to 1991; it says many other establishments have come and gone yet they are still going strong.

The only thing inside the cafe which seems to have stirred since those early days before the First World War is the coffee. The formica tables, the counter, chairs, the strawberry, raspberry and knickerbocker glories, are all part of the enduring appeal of the place for holidaymakers, students, hitchhikers and Portstewartites.

It's now six o'clock. With sufficient luck I hope to get through Coleraine and over to Castlerock for the night. Traffic is heavy coming out of Portstewart but it's half an hour before I get the lift I want. A retired couple, Joey and Margaret Simpson, are out for an evening drive to Castlerock. Joey has tired of tending the lawn, watering the tomatoes and looking after the roses and rhododendrons. He has decided on a drive along the coast.

He says Portstewart is one of those places where it's impossible to get your car parked along the sea front on a summer evening, unless you've had it there since eight in the morning. Castlerock doesn't have the same congestion, and is remarkably free of lager louts. It has a subdued atmosphere for a Saturday night with a few holiday makers pottering about in caravans. I'm dropped off at a caravan park beside a row of cottages which are known as the 'Twelve Apostles.' A neat row of twelve houses in black stone with small dormer windows, they sit quietly out of sight above the railway track – a little part of old Ulster which has been secretly retained in this corner of the north coast.

At one end of the town a memorial commemorates the fishermen who have been lost at sea. It was set up by the Shipwrecked Fishermen and Mariners Royal Benevolent Society which was founded in 1839 for the 'alleviation of every phase of shipwreck disaster among the seafaring population and their dependants.' It has a simple poignant message: *There is sorrow in the sea.*

I enter Love's Bar in search of information. I want to find out about a boat from Magilligan Point tomorrow over to Moville or Greencastle in County Donegal, thus cutting out the city of Derry with its suburbs and roundabouts. Some enquiries reveal the name of Seamus McLoughlin who runs boat trips across Lough Foyle. It's not a regular service but I am told he may be organizing a trip tomorrow morning. A telephone call to Seamus fixes up the arrangement. He tells me to report at eleven o'clock. Weather permitting, he says, he will take me across. Seamus warns though that it can be rough and likens his small boat going across to riding a surf board.

I notice Castlerock is bereft of amusement arcades and leisureland complexes. When I return to Love's a man in the bar says they're trying to discourage what he refers to as 'the yobbo' type of holidaymaker. He says if an amusement arcade is built the local people will burn it down on the first night.

It is the end of a long freezing day on the road in which I haven't covered much ground. But I take great delight in wrapping my hands round a hot port and burning the cold out of my system.

* * * * *

It has rained heavily overnight on the north coast. By the time I get on the road to Magilligan Point the only remaining traces of it are a few puddles. Sunday morning traffic is building up slowly. Five cars pass me before I manage to catch a lift with a couple who are on their way to open their shop near Benone beach.

The owner, Jim McBride, says they've been having a poor summer so far, what with the bad weather and the recession. He says the beach at Benone this year won a blue flag award. Benone beach in fact is the only Northern Ireland beach with European recognition. Blue flag status denotes not only a high standard of environment quality but also the provision of basic facilities and environmental information.

Jim says the beach is cleaned daily during the bathing season and has excellent facilities. 'There is a first aid post, life saving equipment, good changing and toilet facilities and the bins are regularly emptied,' he says. 'It's a very clean spot for bathing and is one of the safest places in the country for swimming.'

Only twenty-nine UK beaches were awarded the blue flag. Jim says the quality of the water is constantly monitored and no sewage discharges are allowed along the beach area. The authorities are even strict about allowing domestic animals on it.

'All dogs must be tightly controlled and kept on leads, and they don't encourage people with animals. It's not very well known about, and unless it's a hot day it is usually deserted.'

Jim drops me on the Seacoast Road near the former Magilligan railway station. My rendezvous time with Seamus McLoughlin is an hour away and I have only to get the four miles from here out to Magilligan Point. A few cars pass with people dressed in their Sunday best for church. The temperature has warmed up considerably from yesterday although it is still not hot enough for sunbathing on a blue flag beach. I'm not unduly worried about getting a lift because Seamus had told me if he saw me on the road he would pick me up.

I see some wild flowers growing at the back of the red brick station house which is now a private dwelling. Here I find wild geraniums with their deep leaves and slightly hairy stems growing alongside the railway line. I recognize the plant from my field guide as meadow cranesbill. It is normally associated with Dunluce Castle and the Whitepark Bay area, but I had not so far seen it. I take several photographs of the flowers and attract the attention of the man living upstairs in the station. He says it is a striking flower and tells me there is a local name for it. It is called the 'Flower of Dunluce,' and apart from some areas of the north coast it is not found anywhere else in Ireland. The geraniums are violet-blue and have five petals on each stalk. I count the number of flowers growing at this spot. There are eleven in total.

I explain my presence to him and why I am prowling at the back of his house. He says he and his wife are going to Limavady and they'll run me out to Magilligan Point.

I arrive at the Point Bar half an hour early for Seamus. The strand ends at the top of Magilligan Point which reaches out into the lough. The beach and sand dunes are deserted and of the eight caravans, only one is occupied. Across Lough Foyle the fishing ports of Greencastle and Moville on the Inishowen peninsula in County Donegal can be clearly seen. It is a choppy morning, and making a crossing by boat I fear could be difficult.

Seamus arrives shortly and gives his verdict. He says the sway is too heavy and we should wait for an hour to see if it calms down. He says it is a difficult lough to cross because of a deep channel in places. There have been many boating accidents and tragedies over the years and he is not prepared to risk my life or his by crossing in rough waters. I agree to hang around to see if conditions improve but I explain that I must cover certain distances each day and cannot wait too long.

I head over the dunes in search of more flowers. I come across a small pink-flowering plant known as seaside centaury which is growing near wild thyme. There are also some purple orchids, and seaside spurge. An hour later back at the Point Inn Seamus is not any more optimistic. He says we should give it another half hour. He tells me of his ambitious plans for starting a car ferry service between Magilligan Point and Greencastle. He says it would be used by lorries and would speed them on their way to Coleraine, Ballymena or Larne for the ferries to Scotland. He has already submitted plans to the local council about the project.

'Making the scheme a commercial success could be difficult,' he says. 'Car ferries generally throughout Ireland are losing money, but I think there could be a tourist spin-off from this one.'

Seamus believes with the arrival of the European market and common boundaries there will be no worries from the customs authorities as the market place will be wide open. There will though still be security considerations as vehicles and passengers cross from the Republic into Northern Ireland. Another thirty minutes pass. Seamus says he will make a final decision about taking the boat out at two o'clock. He is keen to bring me across and like me is disappointed about the conditions.

I am beginning to despair of reaching Donegal by nightfall. I've already lost an entire morning and have travelled just ten miles from Castlerock. I explain my reasons to Seamus for wanting to avoid cities. He is sympathetic. The difficulty for hitchhikers, I explain, is the sheer number of roundabouts and suburbs. Although Derry is not a large city I don't want to end up having to walk through it as I feel that would impede my progress. Seamus smiles understandingly. I tell him I want to concentrate on villages and if possible avoid cities altogether. I have always respected what 'Uncle Mark' said about small towns:

Human nature cannot be studied in cities except at a disadvantage – a village is the place. There you can know your man inside and out – in a city you but know his crust; and his crust is usually a lie.

Seamus serves me a coffee to cheer up my spirits. He says his daughter will be going to Limavady and will put me on the road to Derry. By two o'clock he feels he is still unable to cross so we part company. A case of foiled by Lough Foyle. The road to Limavady sweeps past Binevenagh Mountain. It is known as the Bishops Road because it was built by the earl of Bristol when he was Bishop of Derry. We skirt the edge of Limavady and his daughter drops me on the busy main road leading to the city.

Cars, mostly containing families, drive past at the rate of twelve per minute. Then a Ford Escort passes me and the brake lights appear. Fred McCorry is on his way into the city and agrees to leave me at the Letterkenny turnoff over the Craigavon Bridge. The perfect lift. When I arrive at the Letterkenny Road the hands on the clock of the Foyle Valley Railway Centre say ten past three. Within five minutes I manage to secure one of those lifts hitchhikers dream about; a lift that whisks me more than fifty miles into the north-west highlands of Donegal.

The dramatic change in my fortunes comes about courtesy of Louis Bowen and his mother who are heading off for a Sunday afternoon drive. I had reckoned on getting to Letterkenny or Ramelton, but when they say they are going to Dunfanaghy my wildest hopes are fulfilled. Within a few minutes we cross the border and pass security force signs apologizing for the inconvenience and saying: '*Don't blame us for the delays, blame the terrorists.*'

Louis is an educational welfare officer and covers most of County Derry in his job. He says one of the biggest problems he faces is the high rate of child abuse.

'It's not only in the city itself, but in the rural areas that the problems of incest are so serious,' he says. Within the last five months he has personally dealt with more than thirty cases of child abuse and there are many others that he hasn't been told about or have not been reported.

As we slip through the luscious green Donegal countryside Louis changes his musical selection every so often. From Letterkenny, at the point where Lough Swilly cuts deep into Donegal, we bowl along through Ramelton, Kilmacrennan, Termon and Creeslough. A crowd has gathered to watch an afternoon of set dancing outside cottages in Creeslough and listen to some traditional music. The large flat top of Muckish Mountain comes into view and the individual peaks of the Derryveagh Mountains stretch away into the distance.

I've now exchanged the smooth tarmacadam of the northern roads for the potholed roads of west Donegal. It's a world of dual language road signs. A place with different money, contrasting shops, European-style car number plates and a region where they speak with a softer lilt. Outside Creeslough Louis stops to pick up two girls hitching to Dunfanaghy. They squeeze in beside me in the back seat and say they're on their way to start work in a restaurant. The next twelve miles pass quietly until we reach Dunfanaghy. I express grateful thanks to Louis and his mother and walk off in search of accommodation.

Dunfanaghy consists of one main business street with several hotels and cafes, five pubs and a handful of shops. Groups of young men in their late teens and early twenties sit in cars in the Square where a large map on the gable wall of a house near the harbour lists the fifty-eight most important archaeological sites in the county. It also outlines in detail the national primary roads, the national secondary roads and what it labels, the regional roads which follow the coast at various intervals, south from here.

An architectural guide to the area doesn't mince its words about Dunfanaghy. It says of the town:

The salt air and the fish and chips of the place are more likely to leave a greater impression than are its buildings.

To test the quality of the fish I eschew the tender Horn Head rabbit with mustard and champagne and settle instead for the haddock, fresh from the sea, at the Copper Grill. On Highland Radio Nanci Griffith, Foster and Allen, and Philomena Begley dominate the airwaves. The waitress says the main summer tourist season has not begun yet. In July and August, I am told, accommodation is hard to find. Northerners frequent the area in large numbers during July, but the main attraction tonight is The Bank Holiday disco seven miles away in Falcarragh.

On the way back to my guest house I pass hedges of fuchsia along the roadside. I stop to enjoy the loud persistent tunes of a song thrush while its mate hunts for snails in the garden of a house.

It is the end of a frustrating day, a large part of which was spent hanging around waiting for the weather to improve. But my frustration is removed by having reached Dunfanaghy with the longest lift so far. Tomorrow I'll turn south to try to make as much progress as possible along the west Donegal coast. So far I've covered two hundred miles of the northern coast of Ireland and, taking an optimistic look ahead, have only thirteen hundred miles to go.

SOME LIKE IT COLD

Dunfanaghy to Rossnowlagh

Day Four. I've now settled down to a familiar pattern: the disorientation of a new bed every day and the routine of early morning life at the edge of small towns. A local farmer, Mickey Murphy, picks me up on the Falcarragh Road. Mickey, who maintains gardens in the area, is a keen ornithologist. He talks about the campaign to save the corncrake. A few nights ago, he says, he heard two calling in a field near his house on the Horn Head road. The birds come to the same field each year from their winter quarters in southern Africa. Mickey says there are very few left in Ireland. In 1988 the total number recorded was less than a thousand.

The bird depends on the availability of long vegetation for cover and Mickey says farmers have been asked to take measures to give the corncrake a chance of surviving. The usual practice of cutting the field from the edge towards the middle can trap corncrake broods in long grass and there is no way for them to escape. In many cases the farmers now work in fields using a method that protects the birds. It involves mowing from the centre of the field out to the edges and cutting slowly from one side to the other in strips. In these cases the birds will normally run from the machinery into the safety of a hedge or adjoining field. Mickey says these methods are known as 'corncrake friendly.'

'This is one of the few areas in Ireland where the corncrake can still be heard,' he says. 'The farmers have been trying to help by leaving some areas of rough vegetation on the farm uncut during the spring and summer.'

Mickey says seabirds such as razorbills and guillemots are also declining. 'There are still big numbers of them but a recent survey showed razorbills

23

around Horn Head had fallen from twelve thousand to about five thousand.'

Mickey drops me in Falcarragh and I take up a position underneath some trees harbouring rooks and jackdaws. The village seems to be having a lie in, or perhaps hasn't recovered from last night's disco. Most shops are still closed at ten-thirty, and the main business is centred on McGee's service station and VG shop.

From my hitching spot there are fine views out to sea of the islands lying off the coast. I look at the map. With its jagged edges the coast of Donegal appears to stretch on endlessly. My plan is to get out to Bloody Foreland, through the Gweedore area, then around the Rosses and as far south as I can by the end of the day. For the hitchhiker a bank holiday means different possibilities. On the one hand there may not be much business traffic on the road, but there's a chance of more people on day trips touring the countryside.

A series of three short lifts brings me the ten miles to Bloody Foreland, past the townland of Bedlam. Niall McClelland drops me at Knockfola. He is a painter and decorator and is on his way to spend the day whitewashing his mother's holiday cottage. The sun has now come out and the scenery is stunning. The clouds disappear rapidly giving way to some real heat and the Atlantic takes on a deep sapphire colour. The countryside is covered with dozens of cottages and bungalows. Small stacks of peat are piled at the side of many houses and the landscape is covered with dry stone walls.

When Niall tells his mother, Ellen, about my trip she runs out of the house and insists I come inside for tea and turkey sandwiches. One of the rules of the road for the hitchhiker is never to refuse hospitality. Ellen is originally from the area and is a fluent Irish speaker. Bloody Foreland, she says, got its name from the red hill of blood, which is what it looks like from the sea. After tea she asks Niall to run me another couple of miles to near Derrybeg whose international claim to fame is that it is the home of Sam Spudz, the Irish potato crisps sold throughout the country and made by the Irish Snack Food Company Ltd. The factory is one of the main employers in the area.

I'm dropped about a hundred yards back from the Atlantic. It is calm and still. The perfect place to be stuck for an hour or two at the side of a road waiting for a lift. From Bunbeg, people I meet along the way say it is a busy road to Burtonport and there will be no difficulty getting a lift. I ask one man at a crossroads how far it is. He says it is about fifteen miles, 'but I couldn't say for sure how many kilograms that is.' Traffic overhead is busier than on the road. Three herring gulls circle near me, and then speed off towards the sea. A coach load of Americans on a tourbus The Emerald Isle Flyer pass by. A lift in Paddy Joe's meat van takes me as far as Annagry.

I walk through the village to the outskirts where I stop to chat to a man cutting grass at the roadside. Anthony Aloysius Bonner claims to be a second cousin of Packie Bonner, the Republic of Ireland's 1990 World Cup goalkeeping hero. He says he is over eighty and was a footballer himself in his youth.

'I was very fast . . . a good runner with the ball,' he says with a bright twinkle in his eyes. 'There wasn't a man on the field could catch me. I was like a racehorse. If Jack's Army had me in their team, I think we might have won the World Cup.' He was born on the fifth of January, 1911 and has lived all his life in this area except for brief spells at Nairn and Inverness in Scotland.

Behind me for the past few miles the white conical peak of Errigal, the highest point in Donegal at nearly two and a half thousand feet, has been a constant friend commanding, almost demanding, attention. Anthony has climbed many of the mountains.

'Errigal is a good mountain to walk up,' he says. 'There are two summits at the top with a thirty yard path joining them. There's only room for one person to walk along it at any time, so they call it the One Man's Pass.'

The road to Burtonport is hilly, narrow and twisting. I come upon a football game, where a team of married men are taking on a team of bachelors in an annual bank holiday encounter. It appears to be seventeen a side. The single men, with youth on their side, certainly have the edge and create an opening to put the bachelors three goals ahead. No doubt a few budding Bonners in the making.

The excitement is too much for me. I continue another mile and then rest at the grassy bank on the roadside as my rucksack is too heavy for walking any further. The silence is disturbed only by the loud song flight of sedge warblers. I get the feeling I'm invading their territory. The sound of another bird that I haven't heard for some time greets my arrival in Burtonport – the cuckoo. Five loud clear calls. So far it is a patchy, disjointed day. I give Burtonport a look over and investigate the possibility of a lift to Killybegs in a fish truck. I'd heard from a farmer there are regular runs each evening, but there is some doubt as to whether there will be any tonight because of the holiday.

Burtonport is a characterless untidy collection of a few houses, shops and pubs. Life is concentrated around the harbour and fishermen's co-operative. It is a small community where everybody knows your business or wants to.

The barmaid in the Skipper's Tavern says it's unlikely any lorries will be going out tonight as no trawlers are fishing because of the holiday.

Burtonport has its own quieter version of lager louts. Two drunks, whom she calls Timmy and Eddie, lie in a stupor over each end of the counter – having obviously entered with too much eagerness into the holiday spirit. The barmaid solves the mystery of posters I'd seen on telegraph poles and shop windows. It features a group of musicians under the name Goats Don't Shave. She says they're a new band playing pop, folk and traditional music and have been packing halls and concert venues in recent months. The band is based in nearby Dunglow and one of the leading members used to own a fishing boat in Burtonport called *The Ranger*.

Outside there's a reminder of the sea and the tragedies it brings in a memorial on a slab of rock to the young men who lost their lives at Rathlin O'Beirne Island in the shipwrecks in 1975 of the *Evelyn Marie* and *Caraig Una* in 1976:

> *They are in the hands of God.*
> *No torment shall ever touch them.*
> *Their going looked like a disaster, but they are at peace*
> *Let not their memory perish.*

By ten o'clock the harbour and fishermen's co-op are deserted. A brilliant late-evening rainbow has emerged across the sky, its strong colours standing out against the darkening light. Amongst the small fishing boats though there is no activity, so I cut my losses and check in for the night at a local B & B.

* * * * *

A trickle of early morning rain builds into a steady heavier drizzle as the Aranmore Ferry, *Misveach*, docks. About twenty passengers and four cars disembark. From the pier the west side of Aranmore Island looks dark and eerie, while its east side, particularly Frenchman's Hill, grabs the sunshine.

As I prepare to walk out of the town a Mitsubishi van carries out a U-turn and the driver pulls up to offer me a lift to Dunglow. I'm surprised that Brendan Donnelly picks me up as he is running a mail service for a local company. He works for a private firm which delivers mailbags and parcels to towns and villages. It's probably the safest lift I'm likely to get as we have a *garda* escort out of the village and along the ten bumpy miles to Dunglow.

Brendan says he stopped because he thought I looked as though I had an honest face. The crown of my head touches the padded top of the van several times as we bounce along the road. Brendan is in a hurry to get there. At first I think it is great fun. But as we continue to round corners at sixty or seventy miles an hour I have second thoughts. It seems he's playing a game with the police patrol car behind us. He is determined to try to shake them off, but they maintain their presence keeping a watchful eye on the hitchhiker.

From Dunglow a local man runs me to Lettermacaward. He describes himself as a part-time farmer and talks about the fishing industry and the restrictions on salmon fishing which have been introduced to protect the stocks. He says the main problem nowadays is that fishermen are using monofilament nets which are invisible to the fish and which catch everything that comes along, including big seabirds such as razorbills.

He doesn't do any fishing himself. 'A spot of poaching three or four times a year, but don't tell anybody,' he winks. 'Just enough to get some trout or salmon from the rivers which I freeze until Christmas.'

The infrastructure of Lettermacaward consists of a school, a butcher's shop, two bungalows, and a shop and filling station. I place myself outside the latter in the hope of being in an easily pickupable position. The population of Lettermacaward may be small but its population of midges is enormous. They're attracted, not only by the sunlight, but also by the sweat of armpits and take a tremendous amount of satisfaction from squirming down the back of my neck. How I wish I'd brought that insect repellent I thought I would never need. After an hour of fighting unsuccessfully to rid myself of a plague of the irritating little pests and trying to attract a lift, I walk over the Gwebarra Bridge and position myself in a midge-free area at the far end.

It is a better place for cars to stop and within ten minutes a transit van pulls up. Laurence Gildea is on a delivery run to Maas (pronounced Moss, he tells me) Glenties, Ardara and Killybegs. The very route I wish to take and the ideal lift for a stranded hitcher. He is delivering ham, sausages, bacon and corned beef to shops and I tell him I'll be happy to wait while he continues his business. He says if I'd come last month on my hitchhiking trip I'd have had warm weather as he was driving round most of the time wearing a T-shirt.

In the broad main street of Glenties he parks beside a memorial to the navvy poet, Patrick MacGill. The inscription on it reads:

> *I'm going back to Glenties,*
> *When the harvest fields are brown,*
> *And the autumn sunset lingers*
> *On my little Irish town.*

Glenties has the look and feel of one of those 'little Irish towns' where nothing much has altered since MacGill was born in it exactly a hundred years ago. If you removed the cars parked higgledy-piggledy along the main street, and the electricity cables and telephone wires, the view would be much as it looked in 1891.

Ten miles further on in Ardara it is the same picture. The town consists of one longish street with a sharp turn at the bottom where a bridge crosses the Owentucker River and the road sweeps round to the right. The County Donegal guide says it is an important centre for the manufacture of handwoven tweed, and hand-knits are produced from a thriving cottage industry which has gained a deserved reputation.

The place gets its name – which means '*height of the ring fort*' – from a prehistoric iron age rath perched on a ridge in the valley of the Owentucker River. Laurence says he'll be spending about forty minutes in Ardara before heading on for Killybegs on his last call. Most of the businesses in the town don't seem to have opened yet for the summer season, but a party of Americans from Ohio, are making plenty of noise over lunch in the Nesbitt Arms Hotel. Laurence picks me up again shortly after two o'clock and half an hour later drops me off at Killybegs harbour.

* * * * *

Killybegs moves to the rhythm of seafaring life. The town is built around the harbour which is now the biggest fishing port in Ireland and the centre of the country's fishing industry. Trawlers from many foreign ports tie up here and lorries transport fish from the ten processing factories to restaurants all over the country.

On my trip I want to take a look at the state of the fishing industry in Ireland and this seems a good place to start. At the harbour offices Patrick McGarvey, the fishery officer, pushes his papers to one side and says he'll answer any questions I like to put to him.

He says Irish based vessels normally operate out of Killybegs, but earlier in the year there were several UK boats in port during the mackerel fishing season. At the moment there is a self-agreed closure for two months on herring fishing to allow the fish to breed and to reach the quotas required. There is a fleet of around twenty trawlers fishing for whitefish, and eighteen refrigerated seawater tank vessels.

The Killybegs fishermen go off from here for up to three weeks at a time in some cases. Many head for the Faeroes, north-west of the Shetlands, or the English Channel near France in search of fish. Patrick says the industry is not in as bad a state as is sometimes painted.

'We are in a business where quotas and restrictions are increasingly becoming an important feature of life,' he explains. 'We have restrictions on the amount of fish we catch, on the tonnage of the vessels we use, and by and large, there are no new vessels coming in. The men are frustrated because they cannot get their own boats. They would like to have their own trawlers, but it is a very expensive hi-tech business.'

Another area of grievance for the fishermen centres on the fact that the naval service has become extremely zealous over whitefish boats ignoring technical regulations. Boats have been pulled up for offences relating to such issues as registration and logbooks, or for not having the correct type of lettering for a vessel's name and number. Patrick says some of the fishermen feel the naval vessels would be better employed seeking out the illegal foreign boats around the shores of the country.

Most of the fish caught in Killybegs is exported. 'At the moment the Japanese are interested in roe herring and that is a big market for us,' Patrick says. Other markets include Nigeria, the Ivory Coast, Egypt and Europe, especially Germany and Holland for herring.

In the centre of the town a group of west African fishermen from Ghana and Nigeria huddle under the awning of the Harbour Bar sheltering from the afternoon rain. The men have been in Killybegs for nearly four months and live on their factory ship. When they arrived they expected to stay about six or eight weeks processing and packing mackerel on their vessel. But when the company in charge went into liquidation they were stranded.

One of the men flashes me a friendly grin and we exchange comments on the weather. David Aheto says he knows Killybegs better than his home town of Terna in Ghana. He says the men are bored and don't have much money for any social life.

'We live and sleep on the vessel and it is not very big,' he says. 'I don't like it, but we have no alternative. The social life is good but the Irish girls don't like us because of the colour of our skin. But we like the Irish people as there are many of them in our country doing a good job as missionaries.'

David is looking forward to going home to see his wife and two children. He complains about the lack of money. 'We earn less than forty pounds a week. I could easily earn that much in a week in Ghana but compared to what an Irish or British person takes home each week we are poorly paid.'

David says they were supposed to be paid a bonus of one hundred and sixty pounds but they never got the money. The boat owners ran into financial trouble and now the fishermen have been trying to contact solicitors to help their plight. He doesn't like life at sea all the time. 'I get seasick very easily, but what else can I do for my wife and my family?'

He operates a night watch on the vessel in case there is any drift from the anchorage. When the smaller catch boats bring in the fish to their factory boat they process it and freeze it. David's job involves stripping the fish and putting them into cartons. He says he would enjoy it if he was well paid, but there is no incentive to work hard.

In Melly's cafe, which serves substantial portions of fish and chips, the forecast on the radio warns of continued poor weather throughout the country. The announcer says the British Isles has so far had the coldest June temperatures for fifty-six years. On the cafe's walls hang framed pictures of the fishing fleet lit up at night with the catches coming in off the trawlers. Posters outline the EC fishing areas and fishing rights in Ireland and west Britain. A calendar from the Shetland Fishermen's Association reflects the strong connection with the Scottish fishermen of Lerwick.

The road to Donegal town from Killybegs is a busy one. I want to push on further south and aim to stay at Rossnowlagh. Inside a few minutes John McClean, a quality assurance laboratory technician from Letterkenny, picks me up. His job at the catering college in Killybegs involves testing the quality of the fish. He checks it for possible food poisoning from the health point of view and to see how fresh it is. Most of his day, he says, is spent looking for microbes or bugs.

John mainly deals with oily fish such as herring and mackerel for the overseas market. He says they have to meet stiff EC regulations, and the best quality fish usually goes to France and Spain. They don't seem to worry to the same degree about quality control for cod and haddock which is mostly for the home market. He says the quality of the water along the west coast is very high and extremely clean, and it is a good centre for fishing.

'Farming in Donegal,' John continues, 'is still traditional and has not changed much over the years. We don't have the intensive agriculture that you get across the border which means the environment doesn't have to worry about pollution by chemicals, excess slurry or silage seep.'

John drops me in the Square in Donegal. From here to Sligo the road carries a heavy amount of business traffic and I know it will not present any difficulties in getting a lift. It is six-thirty and I want to reach Rossnowlagh, about twelve miles south of the town, but five miles off the main road.

There are a couple of other hitchhikers on the road – the first competition I have encountered. One of them, a young girl, soon gets a lift. The other, a man, gives up after ten minutes and walks back into town. Some of us though are made of sterner stuff. I know from my experience so far that it is just a question of time before I am picked up. In two minutes I'm on my way with a shirt salesman driving home to Ballyshannon. When I tell him my story and ask him to drop me at Ballintra for the Rossnowlagh road he offers to run me out to the coast.

In my list of guest houses I'd written the name Ardeelan Manor and put a star beside it. I telephoned the woman in charge from Killybegs to say I'd be arriving sometime in the evening and she promised to keep me a room. I arrive in good time, check in my ruck and meet the Malaysian woman called Fun who runs the house. She introduces me to her assistant who is called Felicity.

Rossnowlagh, with its strand stretching for over two miles along Donegal Bay, is a cluster of holiday homes and houses with an hotel and caravan park. In the Franciscan Friary beside Ardeelan Manor a plaque acknowledges that Rossnowlagh was judged the winner of the best small seaside resort in the 1983 tidy towns competition and that it has made a valuable contribution to Irish tourism. A sign says it is known as the 'heavenly cove,' although its name means 'wood of the apples.' The Friary houses the Donegal Historical Society's Museum and has a small collection of prehistoric items such as flint knives, stone axeheads, javelin heads and bronze spearheads.

The route to the strand takes me past the Garden of Peace and I stop to take in the drama of beach, sun, sea and sky. I'm joined for a few minutes by one of the brown-cloaked friars on his way down for his nightly dip in the briny. Flannan O'Brien says he takes a ten minute swim each evening, whatever the weather, all year round.

'You've heard,' he says, 'of Marilyn Monroe and *Some Like It Hot*, well I'm one of those who doesn't mind it being cold.'

Flannan has worked in the Franciscan Order in Italy and many parts of Africa for over forty years, but prefers Ireland to anywhere else in the world. He points to the beach where two young men are messing about on surfboards.

'Just look at that . . . practically deserted. If you could transport this to the Neapolitan or Adriatic Rivieras you would pay for every single grain of sand you use. They charge you there just for sitting on the beach looking out to sea but many visitors, especially the Irish, object to paying as a matter of principle. If you are clever and go far enough along certain coasts in Italy you'll find the entrepreneurial men have not reached it yet and the beaches are free.'

He continues on his Italian theme. 'I'll say one thing for the country though, they do keep their beaches clean, generally speaking. It had got to the stage, when I was there, of cleanliness becoming something of an obsession. But then the difference between there and here is that they don't want to lose the tourists whereas we really haven't got too many.'

Flannan throws his towel on to the rocks and gives me a parting grin. I watch him disappear across the beach, plunge into the waves and swim out through dips and swells.

In the Surfers' Bar the two men I'd seen trying to ride the waves are warming themselves with Guinness. Eric Dorrat and Anton Boonzaier come from South Africa and are on a touring holiday of the west coast of Ireland looking for the best surfing areas. They say they are on '*surfari*.'

They buy me a drink at the bar and we are soon friends. The rollers at Rossnowlagh are too flat for their surfing. The swell for the surf is generated out in the Atlantic, perhaps as far as Iceland and the size of the waves depends on that. Anton says if there is nothing happening in the north Atlantic in the way of wild weather then there'll be no surfing.

The walls of the Surfers' Bar are covered with pictures of what Anton calls 'waves of perfection' which is what they are looking for. Photographs of hard core surfers shoulder hoppin' from Portrush round the west coast of Ireland and across the south to Tramore in County Waterford adorn the four walls.

They have heard from a man in the bar that the best surfing is in County Clare and they will head for the Clare coast in the morning after having a look around the south Donegal area. They are excited at the idea of my trip. Eric says he understands why I want to do it.

'Until a few years ago I'd never been up Table Mountain in South Africa,' he says. 'It is the flat pancake shaped mountain which is one of the biggest tourist attractions in our country. But I ignored it all my life until three years ago when I climbed it with a few friends.'

They talk about South Africa and its problems. Eric says both he and Anton are radical liberals and love meeting black Africans. I tell them they should have spent the night in Killybegs.

The conversation continues until late in the evening. Eric and Anton travelled over from Scotland to Larne and drove to Belfast to have a look at the city. They went along the Falls Road taking pictures of the *graffiti* which seemed to impress them. After meeting and talking to a variety of people they came to the conclusion that there are similarities between the situation in Northern Ireland and that in South Africa.

We return to the subject of hitchhiking. Eric, who has hitched in several countries, says the best colour to wear is white. He says it is a psychological thing from the driver's point of view. 'I always wear a white T-shirt for instant recognition at a distance and people think I look clean, even though I may not smell all that nice.'

Before taking leave of my new chums I make an arrangement that if they see me standing at the roadside in the morning either in Ballyshannon or Bundoran they will lift me. They say they will be leaving around ten-thirty and want to have a look at the surfing prospects at Bundoran before heading along the Sligo coast.

FUNKY FRENCH-MAYO

Rossnowlagh to Killala

My eyes have trouble taking in everything spread before me on the breakfast table at Ardeelan. Seven different cereals, six varieties of fruit juices, a selection of yoghurts, nuts, raisins, cherries and every conceivable type of fruit adorn the table and spill over to a sideboard. Bowls are crowded with apples, bananas, pears, peaches, strawberries, melons, grapes, apricots and much more.

After feasting on the above Fun asks me which I would prefer: a mixed grill or smoked trout? I look up at her and realize she is serious. Although never one to turn up my nose at the prospect of some decent fish, I reckon eight o'clock in the morning is just too early to tackle the ten inch smoked trout which has arrived at the other end of the loaded table.

Fun has arranged that her husband will run me the five miles into Ballyshannon where he takes their daughter to school. From there the next stage of my trip is through the narrow corridor that links County Donegal with the rest of the Republic. After thirty minutes standing in the rain watching cars and lorries trundling past I develop a minor bout of travel despair. It is time, I feel, to reconsider my options.

Basically, I have two stark, but realistic choices: continue my journey, or return home. From here it should be relatively easy to get back to Belfast. As the seagull flies it is about one hundred and ten miles. If I get a lift to Enniskillen I can catch the Belfast express bus and be home in ninety minutes. Tomorrow I could be on my way to Greece or the Algarve where sunshine would be guaranteed.

I quickly cast these wicked thoughts from my mind. I haven't come for sunshine and anyway I have a trump card up my sleeve – the South

African surfers from last night who I'm pretty sure will turn up at some stage during the morning.

In the meantime 'Uncle Mark' provides some amusement. I have reached the point where Tom Sawyer himself is experiencing pangs of loneliness with his friends in the woods:

> *The solemnity, and the sense of loneliness, began to tell upon the spirits of the boys. They fell to thinking. A sort of undefined longing crept upon them. This took dim shape presently – it was budding homesickness. Even Finn the Red-handed was dreaming of his door-steps and empty hogsheads. But they were all ashamed of their weakness, and none was brave enough to speak his thought.*

I feel a degree of empathy with Finn the Red-handed. I'm not homesick or even lonely but, standing on the rainy roadside waiting for a lift, the thought of home-life holds many attractions. My arrival in Bundoran does little to lift my spirits. The man who gives me a lift calls it a 'cowboy town.'

In the north-west guide to *The Buildings of Ireland*, published in 1979, the editors describe it as '*a squalid place with little of interest.*' In the intervening years nothing much has changed. With the best will in the world you could not classify Bundoran as pretty. The aesthetic attractions and visual appeal of the place are practically non-existent, and it seems unable to shake off its image of seaside seediness.

One hundred and fifty years ago it was reputedly the most celebrated watering place along the north-west coast and was a fashionable resort for the gentry. Some of the big homes survive in the area and at Brighton Terrace the Magheray House Hotel is still in business. Posters in the windows advertise Ireland's new recording duo 'Dad and Me' and 'Jivin' Ivan' who is playing next week. The big draw though seems to be *karaoke partytime* with the 'House of the Rising Sun.'

Another poster advertises Waterworld, Bundoran's watersports centre intended to bring in visitors. The huge blue steel structure on an eight acre beach front site, which opened just two days ago, is round the corner from the hotel. Although it is open the builders are still working on it. Posters throughout the town advertise the new holiday attraction with its tidal wave, aqua volcano, tornado slide and water rapids. The opening of Waterworld is at least a sign that the powers that be are trying to do something to improve the image of the place.

I have decided to jettison some of the books I've brought as the rucksack is becoming unbearably heavy. The man in the post office says there are plans to spruce up the main street with money from an urban renewal grant which would transform the appearance of the town. The plan is for visitors to make Bundoran their base while they visit other parts of County Donegal.

I'm anxious to get on the road again and am worried about missing the chance of a lift with the South Africans. At my hitchin' post out of this cowboy town opposite a caravan park on the road to Sligo, a golden labrador limps up and sniffs around my feet and rucksack but doesn't seem to like what he smells.

I am now leaving behind the miles of magnificent unsullied and unpeopled sandy beaches of County Donegal. I look at the map to see where today's lifts will take me. From Bundoran there is a short two-mile section of County Leitrim which I'd never before realized touches the sea. Then the coastal stretch of Sligo wraps itself around the bay and on the map looks a reasonably short hop of perhaps sixty or seventy miles over to Grange at the other end. Ideally I want a lift through Sligo town and along the north coast of the county. As I browse through the Irish tourist board's Sligo guide I am intrigued at the variety of spellings of the towns in the area.

There is Ballisodare for Ballysadare, Tubbercurry for Tobercurry, Easkey for Easky, Bonniconlon for Bunnyconnellan, and Inniscrone for Inishcrone. Next door in County Mayo, to add another element of confusion, they spell it Enniscrone. The tourist board I believe should be commended for, if nothing else, avoiding a standardized world.

As I read the booklet an unsolicited transit van pulls up beside me and stops. Three dishevelled looking men sit in the front seat while in the back a group of eight wide-eyed children fix their attention on me. The window is wound down and two of the three burly men fire alternate questions at me.

Where am I from?

Where am I going to?

What am I doing here?

How long have I been in Bundoran?

Do I want a lift?

I tell them I've often pondered questions myself like 'What am I doing here?', but I hedge my bets and don't supply any answers. I'd like a lift, but not in their van; thanks all the same. The driver asks if I would have a few 'spare coppers' for some diesel. I decide the best approach is to withdraw quietly and the van drives off.

Within five minutes that other set of cowboys, the Cape Town surfers, arrive. As they pull up swinging slightly from side to side in their blue Toyota Hiace van, Eric furiously waves his arm out of the window. I climb through a door into the back, push aside a ghetto blaster, towels, clothes and a cardboard box full of beer cans, and settle myself comfortably on a mattress.

Anton is in charge of the driving while Eric takes responsibility for the drinks or 'tinnies' as he calls them. He passes me a can of beer and opens one himself. They say they have checked out the surf at Rossnowlagh and Tullan Strand near Bundoran, but in both places it was too flat.

Anton calls over his shoulder. 'The waves are one foot high and we need at least two feet or preferably three, so it is really a pity.'

I make them jealous with a description of the breakfast feast provided at Ardeelan Manor. I produce some apples which I'd taken the liberty of bringing and which they willingly scoff. The previous night I had not heard much about their own personal lives so they fill in the details.

Anton is a junior doctor who has been working in London for over a year. Eric has lived and worked as an architect in various parts of England. After his travels he will be returning to 'Mother Cape Town' as he calls it to continue his studies. In London he was an expert on such crucial information as where the best bitters are to be found and in what areas the best independent or 'indie' music can be heard. He has lived in six different areas of London and likes it very much. For Anton it is just too big to come to terms with and he does not want to live there much longer.

They ask me questions about my work and more cans are handed round, this time in exchange for bananas. They say they like what they've seen of Ireland so far, even though they've only been in the country for four days. With slow enjoyment Eric munches his way through his banana. He describes Ireland as 'fun, funky and fascinating.'

The hills of Sligo roll by. We pass Ben Bulbin Mountain and drive through Sligo town. At Ballysadare we turn off the national primary Dublin-Sligo road. Anton and Eric are heading for County Clare but want first to have a look at the Sligo coast. They say they'll take me as far as Ballina in County Mayo.

We drive down a small road to look at the surf coming in over Sligo Bay, but the waves are no more than a foot high. Anton says they need offshore waves, but they are not too dejected. 'It's the same everywhere. Even in South Africa at my favourite spot – Jeffreys Bay near Port Elizabeth – there are many days throughout the year when it is hopeless for surfing. The ideal time of year to come here for surfing is probably in the autumn, but that did not suit us.'

Eric says there are basically two types of surfers: a natural and a goofy. 'A goofy surfs with his back to the wind which is the way I prefer to surf. But I also like surfing to the front side. It is much easier surfing front side to the wind than backside to the wind.'

That phrase brings to mind a poem by Paul Durcan that I'd read in my book of accompanying poetry. In the poem *Backside to the Wind* he muses, through the eyes of a young boy, on what might have happened had the

French succeeded in their takeover at Killala in 1798. I fish the book out of the library in my ruck and much to their delight give them a recital of selected verses:

> *A fourteen-year-old boy is out rambling alone*
> *By the scimitar shores of Killala Bay*
> *And he is dreaming of a French Ireland,*
> *Backside to the wind.*
>
> *What kind of village would I now be living in?*
> *French vocabularies intertwined with Gaelic*
> *And Irish women with French fathers,*
> *Backsides to the wind.*
>
> *The Ballina Road would become the Rue de Humbert*
> *And wine would be the staple drink of the people;*
> *A staple diet of potatoes and wine,*
> *Backsides to the wind.*
>
> *Garda Ned MacHale might now be a gendarme*
> *Having hysterics at the crossroads;*
> *Excommunicating male motorists, ogling females,*
> *Backside to the wind.*

(*Penguin Book of Contemporary Irish Poetry*, 1990. London).

We drive on to Inishcrone, along the east side of Killala Bay and into the crossroads town of Ballina, known as the capital of French Mayo. Here we part company. It has been a superb lift for me. At over eighty miles it is easily the longest so far. We swop addresses for future contact. The South Africans are heading inland to try to get through Galway and on to Clare by the evening. For my part it is time to search out a launderette as I'm running out of clean shirts. I intend organizing a weekly clothes cleaning exercise. I throw the pack off at the cleaners and head off for a rucksack-free walk.

* * * * *

Ballina has the unhurried throb of a provincial town going about its Wednesday afternoon business. Cars move slowly down Pearse and O'Rahilly Streets. Women look in shop windows and stop for a chat and a gossip with friends. Groups of boys with fishing rods stand in doorways and lean on their bicycles discussing their latest catch from the River Moy, and girls from the Convent of Mercy work out their strategy for securing a catch at the Regency nightclub – Ballina's newest attraction.

In Judge Doyle's restaurant the music of Van Morrison and Paul Simon helps brighten up the afternoon. I wish to get to either Killala or Ballycastle and find a bed for the night. Even though it has been an exceptionally good day for mileage I want to stay in a smaller place.

At the Humbert Memorial on Humbert Street, or *Sráio Humbaire*, the inscriptions are written in Irish, English and French. They are in memory of General Jean-Joseph Humbert and '*the other gallant patriots who sacrificed their lives for the freedom of their country after the landing of the French at Killala in 1798*':

> *Well they fought for poor old Ireland,*
> *And full bitter was their fate,*
> *Oh what glorious pride and sorrow*
> *Fill the name of '98.*

From *Bother na Sup* the route leads out to the main road to Killala. About a mile out of town there is a turnoff for a minor road along the side of Killala Bay – the *Rue de Humbert*. I want to get a lift along it, even though it is much quieter than the main road. It is just after seven-fifteen and is turning into a dry warm evening.

I pick up a lift from a local auctioneer, Paul Leonard, who is going to Killala and agrees to drive me along the back road. Paul spends most of the journey shouting at me in a croaky voice. He calls himself a jack of all trades. He is an auctioneer in the cattle-mart and has spent nine hours in the auction ring with only a half hour break. For this reason he has almost lost his voice. He tells me that as well as selling animals he also sells houses, farms, barns, sheds, outbuildings, lean-tos and he adds, 'wherever there is a pound or two to be made or a building to be auctioned I'll act as the salesman.'

Humbert's Road itself has not changed all that dramatically since his day nearly two hundred years ago. But on the first section sixteen modern bungalows stand at the side of the road. Further along are a line of beech and sycamore trees. We pass three ploughed fields and another containing a blaze of yellow Iris flowers known as yellow flag. It is a colourful flower found throughout Ireland in June. The flowers hang on sharp-edged leaves shaped like a sword which Paul says can cut if not handled carefully. He says they were used by country people in olden times for thatching and bedding.

Paul swerves to avoid a dead fox lying in the middle of the road. At this point the road narrows with room for one car only. Grass grows along the middle and it resembles something more akin to a *boreen*. Paul says these type of roads are affectionately called 'dual cabbageways.' For several miles we follow a low stone wall with flowers growing on it until we pass the ruins of Moyne Abbey, a monastic settlement. It was founded by the Franciscans around 1450 and was burned down by Sir Richard Bingham, the English governor of Connacht, in 1590. Paul describes it as a late Irish Gothic foundation. He says many extra architectural features were added to the original building, including a square tower with six storeys and a renaissance door.

By this time his voice has reached a high-pitched crescendo. I tell him not to talk too much and save his vocal chords for tomorrow. We pass the ruins of another Abbey, Rosserk. It was built in the fifteenth century and is one of the best preserved Franciscan Abbeys in the country. Its fate was similar to Moyne Abbey in that it was burned down by Bingham.

Paul says the buildings include a square tower, nave and chancel and an arched doorway. The Abbey is set back from the road several hundred yards. I visualize him setting out the details for sale and taking bids from prospective purchasers:

Franciscan Abbey: impressive ecclesiastical building; period residence of charm and character in prime location overlooking bay; requires some tender loving care and modernization, but offers exceptional views; spacious accommodation with tremendous potential; would suit young couple keen on interior design, restoration, decoration and building work.

The road from here runs pencil straight for well over a mile. Cattle graze in fields on either side and signs on gates warn of trespassing. Paul drops me at the quay in Killala where I check in for the night at Avondale House, with my own view overlooking the bay.

Apart from Dempsey's grocery shop most of the town is closed. Killala hardly deserves the appellation town. It has a population of six hundred and seventy-four. I peer in through the windows of some of the nine pubs. They all look bleak and dispiriting. A couple of young men play pool in the back room of one. The liveliest seems to be the Golden Acres whose walls are lined with more than fifty framed pictures of the filming of *The Year of the French* which was made in the area ten years ago. They depict scenes featuring soldiers in battle, in the water, on the march and on horseback.

The barman says the film was a disaster. 'It was a total flop. They spent hundreds of thousands of pounds on it and many months here, but it didn't seem to take off. I don't know what the reason for that was, but it just did not capture the imagination of the people.'

I ask him why the pubs are doing so little trade and how they all survive in a small place like Killala. He says there is a tradition among old families, who've been established in certain towns or villages, to hold on to the licence. They usually have had it for several generations and do not want to lose it, so they open only for a limited number of hours. A recent survey has shown that there are two thousand pubs too many in rural Ireland, yet not enough in Dublin. The survey said some publicans would be offered pensions in exchange for their licences. The barman says that there undoubtedly are too many pubs chasing too little business in the country but most manage to get by.

I stroll back to Avondale House and take stock of my first week on the road. Tomorrow is day seven and is going to be difficult. I'm aiming to cross the wide open tract of bogland along the north Mayo coast. Traffic will be scarce. Still, I've travelled nearly four hundred miles since leaving home and have not yet been marooned.

CEIDE COAST: A STONE AGE INTERLUDE

Killala to Belmullet

Another day, another bay. From the bedroom window of Avondale House shafts of early morning sunlight slant down across Killala Bay forcing their way through the clouds.

Two short swift lifts – both with schoolmasters on their way to supervise end of term examinations – take me the nine miles to Ballycastle, County Mayo. I'd been urged by Michael Caplice who runs the guest house to have a look at the Ceide (pronounced Kay-jeh) Field project several miles outside the village. The site, which is in bogland, is older than the pyramids and is said to be the oldest enclosed farmland in the world. This is reinforced by both teachers who say it is the biggest ever development in the area and is certain to be a major tourist attraction.

Ballycastle is a village with a population of two hundred people who support thirteen bars. In between the Seaview Lounge, which also dispenses petrol at the top of the sloping hill, and O'Grady's victuallers, purveyors of quality beef, lamb and bacon, there's also a post office, junk shop, a couple of supermarkets, cafes, a B & B as well as a mobile library and travelling bank. Every Friday there's a hairdressers in the Protestant Hall between ten and six. Four of the thirteen pubs also double as grocery shops. The Mayo guide says a growing number of repeat visitors give testimony to the attractiveness of Ballycastle as a holiday base.

Housed in a small building in the main street are the offices of the Ceide project. Huge archaeological maps of the area are on display along with photographs of the flora and fauna. In a back room the girl in charge switches on a twenty minute video which sets out the history of the project and explains its significance. The video opens with some arty

41

photography and camera work, accompanied by haunting romantic music.
A 'voice-over' outlines the details. It is described as the most intact
neolithic settlement in these islands and the most extensive stone age
monument in the world. The stone walls – as I've already heard from four
different sources – are older than the pyramids.

So far the archaeologists have found fields set out in parallel strips
running across the mountain. At its peak the site housed a thriving
community and the people lived a well disciplined existence. The archaeologists have also found a small neolithic hut and pottery from the period
including flints and part of a polished stone axe. One of the most important parts of the find is the charcoal around the hearth of the circular
building. When radio-carbon dating analysis was carried out it was found
that the charcoal dates from around 3200BC.

The video looks at the tourist potential of the Ceide Fields: it is hoped
to turn it into a big development. When the video ends the girl says she
can arrange a tour of the site for me with the archaeologist working at it.
She says there are mixed feelings about the project among local people.
Some believe it would have been better to put the money into a factory to
create jobs for the area, but others are fully behind the concept and want
to see the development taking place as soon as possible.

Noel Dunne, a freelance archaeologist who has been working on the
site for several years, arrives in the office. When I express an interest in
having a look firstly at the bird life off Downpatrick Head he says he is
driving out near the area to deliver equipment. He offers to drop me there
for half an hour, then pick me up and take me out to view the Ceide Fields
in detail. Never mind making progress, I decide, this is too good an
opportunity to miss. Even if I hadn't known, it would be easy to guess that
Noel's Opel Kadette is owned by an archaeologist. A wheelbarrow sticks
out of the boot and I squeeze into the front seat beside spades, shovels and
hammers. The back seat and floor are littered with wellington boots,
muddy shoes and a selection of tools. On the dashboard sit two cream
coloured clay pipes, looking as though they've just been unearthed that
very morning.

Noel drops me at Downpatrick Head where I walk through a thick
carpet of sea pink flowers for a view of the dramatic ragged cliffs. A short
distance out to sea the rock of Dun Briste's limestone cliffs is home to an
array of seabirds including guillemots, kittiwakes, fulmars, shags and herring gulls. Some even have their own positioning quirks. The kittiwakes
keep to the narrow ledges of the rocks while the guillemots occupy the
broader ledges and favour more space. After listening to them for several
minutes it occurs to me the sound is comparable to children playing.

Noel picks me up again and brings me to the Ceide Fields themselves on the other side of Ballycastle. We walk up a hill past areas which have been dug up or excavated and where metal rods are driven into the bogland. Wooden posts mark the spots where further probing is taking place. Noel is totally wrapped up and excited by the project. He floods me with information: statistics, historical facts and recent gleanings.

'It is an exacting and time-consuming job,' he says. 'The people lived here in a cohesive stone age community and the fields were huge. The site was in the region of two and a half thousand acres. The prehistoric settlement was about ten thousand and this hillside alone could have had as many as a thousand people on it at any one time. It was a very big economy. The people had a tremendous knowledge of the sea and were extremely well organized. As you can see from what we have here the field systems were all a regular pattern and they would probably have been used for cattle management. The people ran agricultural activities with nothing other than the stones that they had to hand.'

Over the years the people exploring this site have been stripping back the layers of peat from it to reveal something new about the past.

'When the stone age people lived here it was a forested environment, but the farmland became engulfed by bogland and it is now a completely treeless area. It is believed that the clearance of the trees set off the developments for the rest to happen. It is only in north Mayo that there is evidence for these extensive field systems. At least, so far that is the only area where the evidence has come to light – there may be other places we don't know about.'

Noel brings me over to what he reckons is one of the most exciting aspects of stone age life – the court tombs. There are six of them on the Ceide site.

'This is one of the best examples of a megalithic court tomb in Ireland,' he continues. 'There are more than three hundred of them throughout Ireland but when this one was excavated in the early sixties it was found to be multi-chambered and was built by skilled craftsmen.'

The tomb is about five foot in depth. We step carefully down inside. Noel says when it was uncovered the burial chambers and stone cairn were practically intact. 'This was a communal tomb where men, women and children were buried together. The people were cremated in large numbers and this tomb contained the remains of thousands of bodies.'

He says they found stone age implements and a stone axehead which had never been used and was beautifully polished. We continue our walk over a fence and into an adjoining field. Noel tells me about the plans to build an interpretative centre. It is expected a small portion of the site will be developed and will feature the main important elements of the farming community. The plans are that the centre, hewn from a quarry on the cliff edge, will be linked by a tunnel under the road to the main interpretative centre on the bogland. It will provide information on the geology, archae- ology and botany of the Ceide Fields and on the north Mayo region.

The area is rich in flora and as we make our way back down to the office Noel points out some wild flowers which grow in the bog fields. We come across the oblong-leaved sundew plant which grows in various patches, and the spotted orchid, which has now shed its spots. We also see the pink-flowering lousewort, the milkwort which has blue spiky looking flowers and narrow leaves, and the common butterwort which grows in bogs and wet areas and is mainly found in the west of Ireland. It has a sticky feel to it and attracts flies and insects.

In the distance out to sea are the Stacks of Broadhaven which Noel says are for sale for eighteen thousand pounds. The Stacks, or Stags, are four outcrops of rock lying in deep water about three miles offshore and consist of ten acres in total. Access to them is by boat and is possible only in calm seas. Noel says the auctioneers involved in the sale believe there are several potential purchasers: Irish-Americans, the long-term speculator or investor, wildlife enthusiasts or simply someone with a romantic notion wanting to buy his own island.

We make our way through the fields of bog and grass back to the car. Having spent the whole afternoon at the Ceide Fields I've lost precious hitching time, but Noel runs me to Glenamoy which is about half way to Belmullet.

In the car I ask him how local people reacted to the development. He admits that at the start there was pessimism about it. 'But people are now beginning to see the benefits and the potential tourist spin-off,' he says. 'I think most locals are committed to the idea and I would say we have overcome the initial misgivings.'

He says a dispute is presently going on because land needed for the project could not be bought from a local farmer at an agreeable price. The commonage sought is owned by eight farmers who were offered five hundred pounds an acre by the Ceide Fields committee. Seven of the landowners were prepared to accept the offer but the eighth farmer wanted a thousand pounds an acre which was well above the committee's budget.

Noel says County Mayo is undergoing something of an archaeological renaissance. 'There is an unprecedented level of research being carried out by both professional and amateur archaeologists and the county is at the forefront of landscape studies. In fact the archaeological survey for County Mayo runs into two volumes and it is the only county in Ireland where that is the case.'

On our way to Glenamoy we are in a remote region with bogland on all sides. The colours are mostly browns and yellows. Ahead of us in the distance stand the twin peaks of Tannymore and Tannybeg. Noel says because of their shape they are known locally as the 'Dolly Partons.'

I take my leave of him at Glenamoy, which consists of one pub where we have a drink before parting company. It is now six-thirty. The wide open horizons stretch for miles around. It is desolately peaceful; an isolated and lonely landscape. I think probably the most bleak I've seen since the start of my journey. The countryside evokes a mystical feeling and for those in search of quietude this is the place. I am in search of a lift to Belmullet, some twenty miles away, but the roads are bereft of traffic.

In Ballycastle I'd bought a copy of the local paper, *The Western People*, which claims to outsell the combined totals of all the other Mayo papers each week. It carries a front page article on the hitch over the Ceide Fields site. The paper feels so strongly on the issue that it runs an editorial in which it says the unexpected snag could, if not resolved, limit the potential of a most important development. The editorial continues:

The services of a mediator should be employed as a matter of urgency and no stone left unturned in pursuit of an objective which is far too important to be curtailed in any way. Approached in the right frame of mind, and mindful of the good the development of the site area will have for future generations of local people, we are confident that the impasse *can be overcome.*

The word *impasse* sums up my situation on the roadside at Glenamoy. In forty minutes just three cars pass me. I scan the horizon, my head full of images of how the area might have looked five thousand years ago. I focus my binoculars on Slieve Fyagh which sticks up behind me and on the surrounding countryside. There are no cars, no trees, no fences, no houses and not a single ornithological peep.

There is no doubting the excitement and commitment of those involved in the Ceide Fields development and the amount of local interest it has generated. But in the hills and valleys of north Mayo and along what has become known as the 'Ceide coast,' there are also reservations about the vast amount of money being spent on it.

Some of this is borne out by my next lift. A local farmer, Paddy Hughes, is dismissive of the project.

'The whole thing is a load of bullshit,' he says. 'It's all a lot of nonsense. They have been workin' and diggin' in those shaggin' fields for years and do you know what it is?' he asks me in rhetorical tones as he tries to find fourth gear, 'I'll tell you what it is – it is only bogland and I should know as I've been lookin' at them fields all my life.'

Paddy can't understand what all the fuss is about. He sucks in his cheeks and continues with his tirade. 'When it boils down to it, it is a pile of stones lyin' in a field and if you want my opinion it is all a waste of money. Charlie Haughey is supplyin' them with two million pounds and he has plenty of it, but of course, all he is after is the votes. I believe the money could have been spent on startin' up a factory and givin' more employ-ment to stop people leavin' this area. Instead of that they put the money into one of them interpretation centres that nobody here wants.'

Earlier in the year the prime minister, Charles Haughey – a Mayoman himself – launched an excavation programme of historical sites. His aim was to create thousands of jobs in the industry and in tourism. He said his vision was that scientists should discover the past 'from the moment man set foot in Ireland.'

Paddy sucks in his cheeks again. He deviates and gives me a short lecture on the curse of emigration and how it has blighted the area. He quickly returns to the subject of the Ceide Fields and says he has nothing against people studying their past. 'If they want to spend their time diggin' up fields of bog that is their business, but the ordinary people of this area aren't interested in this. That sort of thing might be all right in other countries but not here. Anyway, they're talkin' about a tourism benefit, but it could be twenty years or more before there is any real return in this area for the local community.'

Paddy drops me in Belmullet and I express my gratitude for the lift. I'm also glad to have heard a smattering of the other side of the Ceide coin.

The dining room of the Western Strands Hotel, where I am the solitary customer for the first hour, has a comfortable innocence about it. My musical tastebuds are entertained with a wonderfully warm medley of local sweet and simple songs from Mid-West Radio. *The Cottage on the Hill* is followed by *The Lovely Leitrim Shore*, *The Hills of Knocknashee* and *The Cabin With the Roses Round the Door*. I have always been a supporter of the 'pro-music in restaurants' brigade, provided it is not intrusive. I feel it an enriching element in a meal, and when dining by yourself it adds a degree of sociability.

After dinner I walk down to the narrow isthmus which connects the town with the Mullet peninsula, and stands between Broadhaven and Blacksod Bay. Twelve hours ago – at nine in the morning – I watched the sun rise over Killala Bay. It is now dipping slowly over Broadhaven Bay.

I've travelled a mere forty-five miles along the north Mayo coast, walked through fields, headlands and open countryside, photographed wild flowers, heard the cry of seagulls, learnt something of the history of the area and met the people. I haven't really gained much ground. But this is what I've come for. As we parted at Glenamoy Noel asked me if I'd enjoyed myself. I certainly had. In its own way it had been an exhilarating day.

THE MAYO MONSOON

Belmullet to Clifden

The landlady in Broadhaven View says, without having to think about it, Belmullet has a population of nine hundred and fifty-six. It has a reputation for being one of the most remote towns in Ireland, but she says the people are reasonably happy with their lot. They get their share of tourists who come for the fishing and boating trips.

Every so often there is also an influx of ornithologists to the Mullet peninsula hoping to see the red-necked phalarope, a rare bird which sometimes breeds in shallow marshes. It is said to have a slender foothold in Ireland and generates much excitement when it arrives. The Mullet is the most southerly colony in the world.

Belmullet's streets have little life about them this Friday morning. Farmers stand around waiting for the travelling Allied Irish Bank caravan to open its door. I have always thought of Mayo as being one of Ireland's neglected counties. It probably doesn't feel that way and the people certainly don't have that perception. My impressions were that the county was not necessarily on the main itinerary for visitors and most people drove through it on their way to such places as Connemara or Achill Island. There are, of course, mountains, lakes, glens and bays aplenty, but it seems to have lived in the shadow of its more illustrious west coast neighbours such as Sligo, Donegal or Galway. The tourism authorities bill it as the '*warm, wild and wonderful west.*' The western regional tourism organisation has an amusing boast that they're a bit behind the times in Mayo – but only because they want to be. The guide describes the area around Belmullet as '*a beautiful wilderness where twentieth century pressures seem like a bad dream.*'

From my hitchhiking spot on the road to Bangor Erris a stiff wind whistles in behind me across the waters of Broadhaven. It passes up through a field of tall buttercups, daisies and thistles. I turn round, stand firmly backside to the wind, and silently wonder where the South African surfers have got to by now. A helicopter flies overhead casting a shadow across the northern end of the Mullet peninsula. The man who picks me up says it is from Irish Lights and is on its way to Eagle Island for a routine maintenance check of the lighthouse. Michael Donnelly is on his way to Dublin for a weekend trades union conference. He represents the Irish National Teachers Organisation and says a big debate is going on over union mergers.

'It is happening generally with more unions coming together for strength in various sectors of industry,' he says. 'In Britain there are plans to merge the health service unions and that will be the trend here too because of the unity it brings. A small union does not have any power in this day and age, and more and more of them are now beginning to see the benefits of coming together.'

I tell Michael about my union, the National Union of Journalists. It has the highest annual subscription of any union in the British Isles, and although it has improved the working conditions of some journalists, it is regarded as being Trotskyite-dominated. The views of rank and file members are held in contempt and the extremists have turned it into a fringe political party, churning out left-wing propaganda. It is also broke. There are proposals for merger with print and broadcasting unions about which many journalists are unhappy and there are growing calls for a more democratic breakaway union.

Michael drops me at Neary's Corner in Bangor Erris and I turn right on to the road to Mulrany. Bangor sits between two hills. Its name means '*the pointed hill place of Erris*.' In front of me stands Knocklettercuss Mountain and on the other side of the Owenmore River is Carrafull. I am now entering the mountainous Mayo region. Inland from here lies the Nephin Beg range and out to sea the peak of Slievemore on Achill Island stands out in the morning sunshine. The peace of the area is broken by the noise of children in the playground of a modern primary school with pebbledash walls about a hundred yards behind me. Boys are throwing balls into a basket and the squabbling is reminiscent of the seagulls I heard yesterday at Dun Briste. Four shrill blasts from a whistle signals an end to the morning's fun and the children disappear inside. Within minutes they are replaced on the tarmac by three jackdaws poking around in a jaunty manner, their beady eyes on the lookout for scraps.

Having some time on my hands waiting for a lift I ruminate about the qualities required of a hitchhiker. I reckon there are three main ones: patience, determination and confidence. Everything comes to him or her who waits, patience usually pays off and I have already chalked up over four hundred miles in my first week. Determination is something you show by looking as if you really want a lift with a keen set face. Confidence comes with the more lifts you get. Every journey, even for only a few miles, is in a sense a confidence booster.

Over an hour passes. From the start I'd identified this road as being difficult; even before I set out, in those early days of studying the maps at home, I reckoned it would not be easy. A few local cars pass me. I try to put all the aforementioned qualities into practice but to no avail. Several cars are full of families. Like the mountain behind me it is a question of Car-a-full. In fact it is a full car which finally stops for me. The vehicle swings over the bridge and the driver brakes sharply. He eyes me up in his mirror and, just in case he changes his mind, I run like the proverbial greyhound out of its cage.

Seamus Beattie, his wife and three children, are on their way to Achill Island. I jump in the back beside his baby daughter, a three year old girl and five year old boy who seems not to like the look of me. They come from Coventry and are visiting relations in County Mayo. I spend the next twenty miles in some intimacy with Emma, the three year old and Tracey, the baby, who is intrigued by the zips on my rucksack.

They drop me at the Mulrany turnoff about a mile from the village. On the way in I walk past hedges of fuchsia and fields of foxgloves. Wild rhododendrons, which seem to thrive in the peaty and acidic soils of the area, grow in abundance in the ditches and fields. In one of those climatic shifts which occur regularly in the west of Ireland the clouds have gone and there is now a strong sun high in the sky. The scene is an oasis of calm and it is turning into a warm balmy day. From Mulrany, across the glimmering waters of Clew Bay, the rocky quartzite cone of Croagh Patrick sticks up in the air, a lone protuberance.

Croagh Patrick is probably Ireland's most famous mountain. An annual pilgrimage is held each year on the last Sunday in July when more than forty thousand people, some without shoes, swarm all over its two thousand five hundred and ten feet. The ritual involves the observation of three stations at which prayers are repeated in a set pattern. For experienced ramblers and climbers it is not really a test of any walking endurance as they point out that there is, in their terms, a 'motorway' to the top; no mountaineering skills are needed as the path leads right to the summit. The Irish mountaineer, Joss Lynam, says Croagh Patrick has been climbed by more people than all the other mountains in Ireland put together.

The road to Newport and over to Westport is much busier. A teacher, Dick Harnedy, picks me up at Mulrany. He is driving to Westport. His family come from west Cork where he was born.

'Now though I'm an adopted Mayo man and would not contemplate ever going back to Cork, and mind you that is saying something which most Cork men would never wish to hear. Cork people don't like to lose their own to any other county in Ireland, but I still visit my relations in the area, so at least I keep in touch with the place. There's a lot happening in the west of Ireland and this region has everything going for it.'

I had thought of stopping for a look around Newport which seems a pleasantly decaying little town, but opt for the eight extra miles to Westport. Dick says Newport has become surprisingly popular in recent years as an alternative to Westport which, during the busy summer months, is bursting at the seams with tourists.

'Newport doesn't have the facilities or attractions of Westport, but it is developing all the same. It is a popular angling centre and is becoming an increasing fancy of the French.'

* * * * *

With its smart boulevard and Georgian houses Westport is far and away the most enticing town in the region. It is charged with a Continental aura seldom found in Irish towns and has a sparkle about it which I've not seen since leaving home. The mixed buzz of visitors and locals give it the feel of an Irish country town injected with a polyglot, not to say honeypot, of tourism. Germans, French, Dutch, Belgians and Italians parade the streets of the town and drive through in their caravanettes, motorhomes and campervans on their way to Achill. Then there are the ubiquitous coach parties of Americans buying postcards and marvelling at the Irish way with words:

'Hey Doreen, what's a *boreen*? I dunno, you better ask Maureen.'

In the Octagon crowds of young people spend Friday afternoon lounging around drinking in the sunshine and lager outside Geraghty's Bar and the Grand Central. They sit at tables under parasols in a scene not far removed from that found on the French Riviera. The tourist information blurb on display says of the Octagon:

The central Octagon is an exquisite piece of town planning. Its central pillar, limestone on an octagonal granite base, has happily had an ill-placed public loo recently removed.

A plaque outside the Railway Hotel in the Mall records the fact that Thackeray resided here in 1842. On the à la carte menu the Thackeray room restaurant offers wild westcoast salmon and Clew Bay mussels. When he came here on his Irish tour Thackeray called the area a '*miracle of beauty.'* He said nature had done much for Westport, and he thought the view over Clew Bay was the most beautiful he ever saw in the world.

At the Clew Bay Heritage Centre at Westport Quay postcards and old photographs from the Lawrence collection show the town as it was at the turn of the century, some sixty years after Thackeray's visit. The building was originally erected by the harbour commissioners in the nineteenth century. It used to house animals prior to their export to Scotland and Liverpool. When it was taken over by the Westport Historical Society in 1988 it had no walls or roof and cost forty thousand pounds to renovate. It now contains a museum, genealogical research facilities, a section dealing with the maritime traditions of Westport and information on the works of Mayo authors. Artefacts and documents reflect the local history, customs and traditions of the county. All the bric-à-brac of the area has come to rest here. A donkey pack saddle sits beside horse cart harnesses, spinning wheels, and butter churns. Pictures in a glass display cabinet show Princess Grace of Monaco on her visit in June 1961. She spent thirty minutes in the two hundred year old thatched and whitewashed cottage off the Newport-Castlebar road from where her grandfather emigrated.

The centre has a collection of fading theatre and circus posters dating back to the 1930s. 'The Flying Colours' were putting on a show of speed and sparkle – for six nights only – in the lecture hall in Westport in March 1934. The most versatile vaudeville company touring Ireland 'The Show Stars' were at Westport in 1938. Their galaxy of all star artistes included comedians, crooners, tap-dancers, acrobats and magicians.

The entertainment provided today centres on the *karaoke* night in the Hotel Westport, bingo in the town hall every Friday and traditional music in the pubs. Fossett's circus, with its performing animals from Chipperfield, is in town and the Charlestown Little Theatre Company is presenting *Buried Child* in the town hall. A big street festival featuring Brendan Grace, De Dannan, the Texas Kellys, and the Celebration Jazz Band is planned for later in the summer.

At the quayside in the evening a couple of boats are puttering here and there. A few venture further out into Clew Bay which is said to contain three hundred and sixty-five islands. The views across the bay are immense. Some islands are easy to make out, others are not so visible. Over the years the scenery and landscape here has been reproduced hundreds of times by professional photographers, painters and amateurs with their sketch pads. The scenes across to Achill Island, which reputedly sees the last evening daylight in Europe, have been captured in many different moods. Portfolios have been compiled which later appear in books or on display in art galleries and studios in Westport under such titles as 'The Essence of Ireland,' 'Evening Light, West of Ireland' or 'Full Moon at Dawn.'

In the back garden of the Tower Bar at the quayside the barman says throughout the months of July and August people queue up to take shots of the sunset. He says he would be a rich man if he charged a pound for every photograph. With the orange sun fading I take my own snap. It is a stunning and dramatic scene. I envisage the developed product, mounted and framed on my wall with a suitably appropriate caption such as '*Sunset Silhouette*' or '*Summer Sunset Over the Bay*'; or later when the bright white stars come out in their hundreds and the moon replaces the sun, another snap entitled '*Moonlight in Mayo.*'

* * * * *

The torrential rain beating down on the skylight window in the attic room of *Ceol na Mara* (Music of the Sea) at Westport Quay wakens me shortly before eight. The peaceful and uplifting scene of the previous evening which I had dubbed '*Moonlight in Mayo*' has now turned into '*Monsoon in Mayo.*' The rain is of that tropical intensity that the west of Ireland specializes in and shows no sign of relenting. I contemplate walking into Westport to sit it out but am sufficiently au fait with the weather to realize that in this part of the world you don't wait for the rain to stop unless you have all day and all night. I don't have that amount of spare time on my hands. As I mull over the situation at the door of the guest house a couple are loading their bags into the boot of their car. The driver, a ginger-haired girl called Noleen, offers me a lift to Leenane at Killary harbour which is the direction I wish to go.

The road to Leenane takes us through Louisburgh and past Croagh Patrick now shrouded in a bank of mist and sea fog. The one wiper that is working on the driver's side of the fifteen year old Mazda is having extreme difficulty coping with the rain hammering against the wind-screen. Noleen, from Dublin, is showing her Parisian boyfriend, Bruno, some of the sights of the west coast. He is suitably unimpressed with the rain and in particular with the leaking window in the car where drops fall steadily around his legs and feet. There is also a leak in the back window giving me a gentle shower every so often. I am not complaining though. Anything beats standing outside on a day like this trying to hitch a lift.

From Louisburgh we swing left down through a wild and remote moun-tain road taking us over the Doo Lough Pass. For most of the twenty mile trip to Leenane there are no houses, nor even a trace of one. We pass several cars with their headlights on. It is half-eleven and the visibility is so poor that it makes our progress very slow along the narrow twisty road. The car sways from side to side in the fierce wind which looks as if it might reach hurricane proportions. Noleen has to concentrate on keeping the car on the road as there are dangerous drops on either side.

To our left on the lower slopes of the Sheeffry hills even the sheep are sheltering beside clumps of gorse. Others try to burrow under lumps of rock in search of protection from the pounding rain. The waters of Doo Lough, at the foot of Mweelrea Mountain, are in a choppy mood and it is with no small sense of relief that Noleen eventually pulls the car to a halt in Leenane where we go into Hamilton's foodstore in search of tape.

Leenane has been put on the map as the place where the John B. Keane play, *The Field*, was filmed in 1990. The film dealt with life in rural Ireland in the 1930s. I stop for a look around wishing to stay inside until the rain subsides. After buying Noleen and Bruno coffee in *The Field* coffee shop they drive off. On the walls sixteen black and white framed pictures show some of the highlights from the film. A few doors down in The Field Bar more photographs of the stars of the film including John Hurt, Richard Harris and Frances Tomelty line the walls. The bar is at the back of a grocery store. Several men sit on stools drinking pints or half pints of Guinness. Conditions outside are gradually deteriorating with the rain becoming heavier. Clouds completely cover the surrounding mountains. I try to identify some of them from the memory of a previous visit and from my map. Across the harbour lies Mweelrea and Ben Gorm; inland to the east are the peaks of Devil's Mother and Maumtrasna, and Leenane hill rises steeply behind me leading into the range of the Maumturk Mountains.

I want a lift to Clifden and reckon I'll stop there for the night, and classify the day as a wash out. Back in Hamilton's grocery shop cum pub I keep an eye out for any passing drivers stopping to quench their thirst. On the walls more pictures of *The Field* hang between details of boat trips to the Aran Islands and a poster about the sheep and wool festival in Leenane. The Oughterard Show Society's regional final of the Scotch Blackface all-Ireland ewe lamb championship is also advertised. Another big attraction is the forthcoming sheep shearing competition and sheep dog trials, with associated activities, such as tossing the sack and a 'sheep dance' at the close.

A man supping a pint at the bar says the past winter was one of the worst ever in local people's memories.

'It was a total bastard,' he says. 'We had winds of up to a hundred and twenty miles an hour along the coast. Many parts of it were washed away and at Ballynakill harbour the storms wreaked a great amount of damage.'

He wipes his mouth with the sleeve of his jacket and grins. 'It would really be more of a surprise if we didn't have cold wet weather in these parts most of the year. Mind you May was a good month. You should have come here then for your walk.'

The woman serving behind the bar joins the conversation, and gives me her views on *The Field*. She says if the film had won an Oscar it would bring more visitors to the area but because it didn't, she can't see it attracting many people to come. The man says at least the film brought outsiders to the area, and it was a change from people talking about Dallas or Dynasty.

The *Bus Éireann* service to Clifden stops outside the shop. I resist the temptation to jump on board and hang around inside in the hope of managing to scrounge a lift from someone passing through. That hope is fulfilled when a couple from Strabane call in for a drink and I engage them in conversation. They don't seem to be sure where they are going but conclude that Clifden offers the best prospect. On the way we pass Kylemore Abbey looking striking in the mist and rain. We go through what 'Uncle Mark' might have called the '*almost invisible*' villages of Letterfrack and Moyard before reaching Clifden which, with its spires, seems practically a metropolis.

Clifden is under siege by water. Rain is swirling around the town and rushing down the streets. Overflowing gutters are unable to cope with the deluge. On the menus chalked up on blackboards outside the Central Hotel in main street the offerings are barely discernible. The fresh Clifden Bay lobster is running into the grilled Connemara scallops and seafood chowder. The prospect of some warm chowder seems inviting.

Forlorn looking cyclists touring Connemara stand in doorways in their brightly coloured anoraks and wet weather gear. They clearly aren't enjoying their drip-dry holiday in Ireland. Nevertheless the business of the town continues in the late afternoon rain. The front doors of Clifden's wet face are painted vibrant primary colours: dynamic reds, Prussian blues, fiery yellows and crab pinks. The main street has a solid businesslike appearance. Craft shops, crammed with souvenirs, co-exist with Walsh's food market, Conneely's butchers, and Pryce's tackle and hardware store. Locals mix with tourists in the cafes and pubs. They both seem to have an equally keen interest in the Knock pottery, Celtic glass, and boxes selling Grow Your Own Shamrock.

I'd thought about trying to get further along the coast, possibly to Roundstone, but I am so fed up with the rain I check into a guest house in the main street. I peel off my wet clothing and delight in the luxury of a hot shower and warm towels. By seven o'clock the rain finally relents – eleven hours after the heavens opened in Westport. Clifden is said to be one of the wettest places in the British Isles. More than fifty inches of rain fall in it annually. I'm convinced at least forty-nine of them fell during my visit.

SMASHING UP THEIR SUSPENSIONS

Connemara to the Aran Islands

'Cósta Conamara' [sic] as it's labelled and spelt by the tourist board is a rugged stretch of coastline with large loops overlooking the Atlantic. From the start I had my doubts about the volume of traffic on the roads through it. Judging by the potholes the stretch leading out of Clifden to Ballyconneely looks the type of road to discourage traffic.

After almost an hour I know my reservations are well founded; traffic to Roundstone this Sunday morning is all but non-existent. Nevertheless the rain has stopped and I am content to wait. After all, this is why I'm making the trip. I take long breaths of the salt-tinged Connemara air and revel in the quietness of it all. The area is a little world on to itself with its own private time scale. The tourist guide acknowledges that life moves slowly:

> *In Connemara one soon learns that time is unimportant. Even the ceremony of drawing a pint of Guinness can take five minutes and the man who cannot spare the time to watch this solemn ritual has not learned to savour the important things of life.*

The Church of the Holy Family is drawing in the crowds. Women in high heels step over small puddles on their way to eleven-thirty mass. After sixty minutes of what I term the 'Ballyconneely blues,' and just as mass ends, my salvation comes from a lobster fisherman, Michael Burke from Bunowen, who is going to Roundstone. He says the lobster fishing business is not very lucrative but it is better than fishing for trout. There has been a serious problem in the Galway Bay area with sea trout believed to be damaged by lice, returning to rivers.

'The anglers won't see a decent run of sea trout in the rivers in this area for several years and there could be a total collapse of sea trout fishing here,' he says. 'The numbers have already been reduced from thousands a year to hundreds or even less. Mind you there is another reason. Many people blame the growth of salmon farming in coastal bays and estuaries for the decline in the sea trout, but nobody has yet come up with a solution.'

During the journey Michael talks about a controversy surrounding the beach at Dog's Bay near Roundstone. The Italian state electricity board wanted to buy thirty tons of sand from the beach for use in engineering research in Milan. The excessively white quality of the sand at Dog's Bay with its fine carbonated characteristics is unique. However, some local people objected when the authorities in Dublin gave the Italians the go ahead to take the sand. They mounted a twenty-four hour watch on the beach to make sure none was taken. The local community council was also closely involved in the protest. The beach at Dog's Bay and the adjoining one at Gorteen Bay were devastated in the storms earlier in the year and there was widespread erosion. Since then major work has been in progress to save the dune system, and special seaside grass from the Belmullet area was replanted in the dunes.

'The storms of the fifth of January were possibly the worst that local people can ever remember,' Michael says. 'There were waves of up to a hundred feet in some places. Whole acres of land were lost to the sea and there was a lot of damage to the pier. Because of this a local county councillor said if the Eye-talians wanted the sand from Roundstone beach so badly then they were welcome to it, provided they gave us the stones from the Colosseum to rebuild the pier.'

Michael drops me with a smile and a wave in Roundstone where the rain has returned with a vengeance. From the comfort and warmth of the lounge of Vaughan's Hotel I look out on the main street and the lifeless harbour where five boats are moored restlessly. The weather appears to have settled into a pattern of gusty swirling rain every fifteen minutes or so. Over a coffee I unfold a one inch map of Connemara which I'd bought in Clifden. It was published in 1990 by Tim Robinson, a Yorkshireman who came to live in the area nearly twenty years ago. Spread out before me on the table in the lounge I plot my route through Connemara. I lose myself for half an hour in the absolute maze of meticulously mapped roads which seem to lead everywhere. All the known archaeological monuments and treasures are on the map. An abbreviation which crops up many times is CBG. It stands for 'children's burial ground' and I count more than twenty of them dotted over the map. It is a masterpiece of topography and presents a fascinating study. There are enough roads here to keep you busy walking and hitchhiking for thirty days and there still would not be enough time to cover every byway or *boreen*. In fact it took Robinson seven years walking and cycling to map the region.

It is now one o'clock and the rain has stopped. I pack the map into my rucksack. My feet are itchy again. The roads of Connemara are ahead and I am impatient to be on them. My plan is to hitch round the coastal loops and try to get to Rossaveal by this evening. From there I can catch a boat in the morning over to the Aran Islands, and then jump on another ferry to County Clare, thus eliminating Galway city. If there are no lifts on the coastal route I will contemplate an inland alternative through Maam Cross.

My third lift of the day is in the back seat of a hired Ford Escort with two Germans who are going from Roundstone to Toombeola and then heading inland. A local lift twenty minutes later takes me to Cashel, and I walk a mile and a half to get to the main road to Glinsk. Two Connemara ponies and a few Hereford cattle constitute the main life at this T-junction. Bunches of large pink dog roses grow along the road. Dry stone walls and stony fields give the landscape a grey-green patchwork effect. The botanist and geologist, Robert Lloyd Praeger loved the region and wrote eloquently about it in his best known book on Ireland, *The Way That I Went*.

On a day of bright sky, when the hills are of that intoxicating misty blue that belongs especially to the west, the bogland is a lovely far-reaching expanse of purple and rich brown: and the lakelets take on the quite indescribable colour that comes from clear sky reflected in bog-water, while the sea-inlets glow with an intense but rather greener blue. On such a day the wanderer will thank his lucky star that it has brought him to Connemara.

(Praeger, Robert Lloyd. *The Way That I Went*, London. 1939).

Unfortunately this is not such a day. The peaks of the Maumturks and the Twelve Bens are enshrouded in mist and the rain is re-emerging. One of the Bens – Benlettery – is living up to its meaning: 'mountain of the wet hillside.' I feel a twinge of fraternity with Praeger when he writes of the wanderer thanking his lucky star about being in Connemara, and despite the wet weather I am enjoying my semi-nomadic life. Part of the great adventure is not knowing where I'll be spending the night. I have been an itinerant for ten days and although the road is sometimes hard, and occasionally lonely, there are compensations: the moving pageantry of the clouds, the smells of the ocean, the murmur of mountain streams, the invigorating air, and crossing the paths of ordinary people.

Within a quarter of an hour I'm on my way, picked up once again by a German couple holidaying in Connemara. The road here is known as *Cois Fharraige* which means 'beside the sea.' I hop into the back and provide them with some entertainment as we skirt by lakes and stone walls during the twenty-five mile circular route that takes in Kilkieran Bay and Derryrush.

The discussion centres on the lashing rain blowing in again from the sea and the potholes along the road. They say the holes are not nearly as bad as the ones in what was the former eastern Germany. I produce a newspaper cutting from the *Irish Times* which I'd kept in my rucksack, and read them some excerpts from a poetry competition on Ireland's infamous potholes.

> *The pothole is a wondrous sight,*
> *The best of our inventions,*
> *The tourists come from far and wide,*
> *To smash up their suspensions*
> *The breeding pattern of these things,*
> *Is almost irreligious,*
> *Each one you see, will soon have twins,*
> *They're really quite prodigious.*

And another one . . .

> *Bumpity, humpity, tumpity – crunch,*
> *Think my back axle has gone for its lunch,*
> *Bang, boom, crumpity, hope we don't crash,*
> *Driving down this way is costing me cash.*
> *Potholes a fact of life?*
> *That can't be true*
> *Would someone please tell me*
> *Just who I can sue?*

Potholes aside the journey is a reasonably pleasant one. The Germans are heading for Maam Cross and drop me at Scrib on the turnoff road for Rossaveal. The rain has returned. As I head to take shelter under trees a car pulls up and a young English couple on holiday from Brighton take me to the departure point for the boats.

Rossaveal doesn't appear to have a central heart. It is a collection of buildings with a few shops, a pub, a scattering of modern bungalows and the ferry terminal. It turns out there is an evening service to the Aran Islands and the next boat will be leaving at six o'clock. As I am an hour early for the sailing I opt for a change of plan having exceeded my expectations of getting to this point so quickly and decide to push on for the islands tonight. On my way to the pier the Aran Shuttle Flyer from Galway drives past me taking people to the ferry. In a field to my left a grey heron, its peace disturbed by the bus, flies out of the undergrowth. Lifting, it tucks in its neck and moves off ponderously to another clump of grass in the far distance.

On board the Galway registered *Rose of Aran* about thirty people are making the hour long crossing to Kilronan on Inishmore, the biggest of the three Aran Islands. The boat is full of young people with rucksacks. As we leave Rossaveal a great black-backed gull follows us out of the harbour and stays on our trail, like a predator, for about a third of the trip across Galway Bay.

The crossing is a rough one. A party of ten teenage girls seem to be enjoying the early part of the swell and the thrill of being soaked by foam but after fifteen minutes those not sleeping on the hard red wooden seats are sick. During an Atlantic crossing in foul weather 'Uncle Mark' fell victim to seasickness. Afterwards he described the experience to a friend and said there are too distinct stages:

At first you are so sick you are afraid you will die, and then you are so sick you are afraid you won't die.

Despite its name the *Rose of Aran* is not a sweet smelling vessel and facilities on board are basic. The seats, or more accurately wooden slats, are certainly not designed for comfort. The toilets have a tidal ocean all of their own. It is not a trip for the faint-hearted or squeamish. Halfway across a man comes round whistling with a mop and bucket and puts a bright face on the proceedings. He gives me a nod. 'I hope you're not the seasick type,' he says. I ask him if all crossings are as turbulent as this one. He describes the conditions as 'fresh.'

'The wind is raising a few white horses out there, but this is nothing compared to conditions in the winter.' He smiles. 'We get used to it, I suppose, up to a point.' He goes on with his slippery and unpleasant cleaning task as the boat continues to lurch and dip for the remaining thirty minutes.

In my tourist information guide there is a section dealing with the best method of travelling in Connemara. I'm not quite sure if it's meant as a joke but written in bold black letters on the page with the headline 'Travelling Around' is the following prosaic sentence:

The ferry trip from Rossaveal to the Aran Islands should not be missed.

Obviously the writer never travelled on this ferry. I glance outside where the sea is heaping up more white foam and the swell is getting higher leading to incessant moaning and groaning from the party of girls. I sit with my eyes closed, arms crossed and, like the Lady Affreca, 'think of home.'

There is a general feeling of relief when we dock in Kilronan harbour. Even a couple of herring gulls who had hitched a ride on the boat for the last ten minutes of the journey have a seasick look about them. I had been given the telephone numbers of some guest houses on Inishmore by the tourist board in Clifden and phoned one known as Gilbert Cottage in Oatquarter, four miles away. The owner, Stephen Dirrane, says he has a single room left and will keep it for me. I'm now faced with a minor dilemma. There are only a couple of dozen cars on Inishmore and there is no point in trying to hitch a lift. So I get round the problem by hiring my own wheels – two of them, from one of the island's many bicycle hire shops. I reckon I'm allowed to waive the rules about transport as I am not on the mainland of Ireland.

* * * * *

By 10.30 am the girl in the tourist information office in Kilronan is harassed. She is being pestered with questions about the boat to Doolin in County Clare. She tries to explain to a group of smiling Japanese that there is not necessarily a regular timetable and the ferry will not be sailing again until Wednesday at the earliest. I absorb this eavesdropped information with dismay. The only option for me now is to try to get into Galway Bay on the next boat which isn't until half past four and then hitch out from Galway down the coast of Clare – the very thing I'd hoped to avoid.

With six hours to kill I explore the island on my five-speed machine and cycle over to the stone fort of Dún Aengus. The fort is perched on the cliff edge and is described as one of the most important prehistoric monuments in Europe. Despite the hordes of visitors scrambling over its walls and stones it is remarkably well preserved. The remains consist of three dry stone ramparts and part of a fourth enclosing an area of eleven acres. During the nineteenth century considerable alterations were made when the buttresses in the inside wall were erected.

Inishmore is an ancient landscape. For generations the island's way of life remained unchanged, but change has now come and is continuing to come. For the islanders, life has been transformed since Robert Flaherty's classic film *Man of Aran* was made in 1932. It is shown three times a day during the summer in Kilronan. Since the film was made though electricity, machinery, cars, landrovers and racing bikes (the latter much to the consternation of the jarvey men who run the pony rides) have all arrived. Nowadays dishes for receiving satellite television are attached to the gable walls of houses and bungalows, each island has its own airstrip and the days of the thatched cottages and women in shawls are gone. The young men who drive the minibuses say they would be unable to operate without their cellnet telephones.

For all that though it is a peaceful and gentle land. From the window seat of the American Bar overlooking the harbour the scene is one of serenity and calmness. Youth hostellers lie in the warm afternoon sunshine; children dip their toes into the water and run back to their parents; herring gulls nibble seaweed; the shop assistant from the Aran Island Handicrafts stretches out on a bench with a coffee; a woman with a Maeve Binchy paperback and a towel over her head lies against the wall at the shingle beach; a golden spaniel runs off to retrieve a stick thrown into the water; men tinker around in the *Newfyne* and *Slainte* boats, and the Doolin ferry, *Tranquillity*, is firmly anchored. It looks as if it has no intention of moving for the rest of the week at least, if not for the rest of its days.

It is an entirely blissful scene but in a few moments the quietness of the afternoon is shattered. Suddenly a man throws open the door and strides into the room. He announces his presence for everyone to hear and see. He orders a double Black Bush and a packet of twenty Players cigarettes. He addresses the customers with a trace of a French accent. 'I am ze capitaine. I am a hustler and want a business challenge.' Everyone in the bar ignores him. He looks at the barman. 'Northern Irish whiskey I like very much indeed – it is top class. When I drink it I am very 'appy.'

The newly-arrived man turns to face the customers again and repeats his challenge. They continue to ignore him. Some look at the floor, others chat amongst themselves and a freckled ginger-haired youth sitting on his own at the bar sniggers into his beer.

The man, who looks about thirty-five, is wearing a blue shirt with white spots and rolled up sleeves. Over that he has an open black waistcoat, grey crumpled flannels and a pair of black shoes with no socks. He has a moustache and a small beard that is not quite a goatee. His face has a reddish puckered look and his blue eyes show traces of bloodshot. He holds himself excessively erect; slung over each shoulder is an expensive looking Nikon camera. As he lights his cigarette the match shakes. He looks the barman up and down disdainfully and orders another double Black Bush. For the third time he repeats his challenge and throws a pile of ten pence pieces on to a table.

He spits out his words volubly across the bar. 'I am ze capitaine and I 'ave come to play someone poker for money.' He pauses. His eyes survey the ten customers and fall on me. I am reading the paper intently and try to be inconspicuous. His pontificating is now arousing some attention. Two men sitting at a table near me accept the challenge and he transfers his gaze to them and emphasizes his words with an extravagant flourish of his arms. 'I am an honest man. I say zis before I play, but I play only according to ze international rules and regulations of ze game of poker. Ah . . . now I will open with twenty pence.'

The men sit around the table keen to start the game and throw out their money. The captain sits and then quickly rises to his feet. He goes to the bar and orders an Irish coffee for himself and a pint of Guinness for a man sitting on a high stool. He unfolds a fifty pound note from a roll of money and hands it over.

Before returning to the game he tells the assembled company that he comes from Brittany 'which is a province of France, the same as Ulster is a province of Britain.' He repeats his liking for whiskey and takes another mouthful of it.

There are a couple of bursts of laughter. Then the bar goes quiet as people fix their concentration on the game. The captain counts out the cards: '*Deux, trois, quatre, cinq, six, sept* . . . ' He continues up to twenty-one. The game progresses and the men lose. The captain stands up and begins another monologue. 'Ze capitaine, he hates to lose, he hates very much to lose and he can be a bandit with weapons when he loses.' Pointing to his cameras hanging over each shoulder he says, 'these are my shotguns.'

By this time the owner of the bar has arrived and is decidedly unhappy at the obstreperous customer who has already frightened off a family. He grumbles to the barman about him. He says he warned him about his behaviour last night and will not tolerate any abuse in the bar. He asks him to keep quiet and threatens to throw him out. The captain sneers at him. He is quite unruffled. He lifts his Irish coffee from the counter and with a shout of 'allelujah' takes his first sip leaving a large amount of froth on his moustache. 'Zis is perfection,' he exclaims.

He makes his way over to me again and asks where I'm from. He brings his face closer to mine and fixes me with a penetrating stare. I return a steady look. He asks me to write my home address on his arm where he already has an assorted collection of drawings, addresses and diagrams. I tell him I'm from UKOGBANI. He shoots me a sharp look and walks back to the card game wearing a puzzled expression.

There follows another soliloquy in his slow but stylish manner. He says he is not a good loser. 'I hate to lose. You know Toulouse? That is a city in France but I am not from Toulouse, I come from Paree. Ha! Ha!'

The barman whispers under his breath to a customer something about a 'total gobshite.' He looks up and points at a sign hanging behind the bar above bottles of Crested Ten, Paddy and Mulligan. It says: *'Everybody has a problem, but nobody wants to hear about it.'*

The owner reappears and is becoming more agitated. He tells the captain to sit down and says he has had enough of his tomfoolery. Another game of poker ensues and the Frenchman loses.

'They beat me,' he cries. 'They beat me with a pair of twos. I hate to lose.' He rises up again and shakes his head several times. 'General de Gaulle said that losing the battle is not losing the war.'

He begins a song which is incomprehensible but is something to the effect that 'cocaine and his baby are his love for ever.' He places an order for another drink at the bar. This time he wants to buy a bottle of Black Bush, but his efforts are in vain. The barman won't hear of it. A short heated exchange takes place.

'I can't sell you any more drink. I've told you that already.'

'Why not? I 'ave ze money and like to be 'appy.'

'I think you've had more than enough for one day.'

'It's a crazy place . . . with crazy people.'

He bursts out laughing, but his face instantly changes to a scowl when the island's two policemen arrive. Clearly, the owner has had enough and he calls the police. The captain shouts out a few more loud phrases. 'Vive La Republic . . . Vive La France.'

Fittingly, these are the last words that utter from his lips in the bar. A *garda* produces handcuffs and asks the man to come quietly. They march him out smartly and he is bundled unceremoniously into the back of their red Renault Four and taken to cool off in the cell for the night, bringing to an end an afternoon of high drama and free entertainment in the American Bar.

The captain of the Galway Bay ferry is a much more level headed character and doesn't appear to have had any of what 'ze capitaine' has been drinking. The boat is packed with French and Japanese who've spent the weekend on Inishmore. The journey takes ninety minutes and is a much gentler crossing than the outgoing one. As we arrive in Galway docks a herd of swans line up as if to greet us. I count a total of twenty-one white creatures – a right royal twenty-one swan salute for our vessel.

I am now in the position I wish to avoid: trying to hitch out of a city. As I walk out of the docks along a curving road which will take me on to the main route to Oranmore and down the coast to Clare, I hitch a couple of passing cars imagining it to be a waste of time. To my surprise a man stops. He is a deaf mute. I point to the map showing him Oranmore and he motions to the passenger seat.

On the way out of Galway we pass a total of NINE hitchhikers ranged at intervals along the side of the road – the very reason I choose to stay out of cities. This is the main route to Dublin from Galway and I realize how lucky I have been to secure this lift as etiquette would have demanded that I would have become the tenth person seeking a lift out of Galway. For that reason this is the best lift yet, even though it is only ten miles. There's also the fact that, for the first time, I don't have to talk to anyone or explain what I'm doing or where I'm going. We pass housing estates and half a dozen sets of traffic lights before we reach open country. The journey slips by in a quiet reverie until we reach Oranmore where I take my leave and mouth my thanks.

Almost immediately I'm picked up by a smooth looking Galway yuppie in a Nissan Bluebird, complete with in-car CD and carphone. He is going along the coast to Kinvarra and when he drops me there half an hour later he says I should have no difficulty getting on to Ballyvaughan in County Clare.

The vehicular traffic on the road seems to have subsided for the evening. I spend most of the time keeping my eye on a pair of blackbirds which are nesting low down in trees opposite. They make occasional trips to forage for food. Less than a hundred yards away, and from their roost in the eaves of a small two storey house, starlings are busy trying to imitate the blackbirds' call. Through my binoculars I notice the grey wall has acquired a whitewash of droppings at the entrance to their home. Starlings, well known for their mimicking qualities, have a knack of capturing the sound, not only of birds and other animals, but also all manner of countryside noises.

I seem to have lost my knack of capturing lifts and after forty minutes I give up the attempt to cross the county border into Clare. I opt to spend the night beside Kinvarra Bay, content that I've managed to out-hitch a hustle of hikers, the first major competition I've so far encountered on my expedition.

KERRY KARAOKE

Kinvarra to Ballybunion

The first thing I know the next morning in Kinvarra is that I am developing a severe cold. The symptoms are a sore throat, blocked nose and limbs which ache all over. The household has an early awakening when Mrs. Walsh shouts to her daughter not to forget her umbrella. Her daughter doesn't hear the advice which is repeated in a louder and more insistent voice. From the comfort of my three bedded room in *Coin Cuain* (Beside the Bay) I pull back the curtains and the worst is revealed. The locals call it soft rain and, accompanied by a howling gale, it is sweeping in over Kinvarra Bay.

The combination of the Aran Island outward bound ferry trip and a succession of dank days have all contributed to the development of my head cold. Under the protection of the awning of Fallon's Spar shop at the edge of town I spend sixty shivering minutes waiting for a lift to Ballyvaughan. When the rain stops a clamour of rooks celebrate with a raucous party in trees across from me.

To occupy myself I study the map and leaf through the Clare guide. The county is surrounded by water. In the north, Galway Bay looms over it; to the south lies the Shannon Estuary; Lough Derg is on its east side and the Atlantic pounds it from the west. It's a pity I wasn't able to arrive by boat. Another journey by water though would have exacerbated my cold and might have killed off the remainder of the trip.

The attractions of the county are well known with the Burren plateau and Cliffs of Moher bringing visitors in large numbers. Clare also styles itself as the music capital of Ireland. Every year tourists throng places such as Ennis (*a traditional music centre*), and towns along the coast like

Lisdoonvarna (*the place where the 'craic' was really invented*) and Milltown Malbay (*a major traditional music base*). The information in brackets is supplied by Shannon Development which has responsibility for selling tourism in the region. Their brochure sustains the musical theme with its description of the coast and countryside:

> *Nature has provided a complex symphony of rugged cliffs, serene golden beaches and quiet coves, purple mountains and rich green pastureland.*

A few cars and a CIE Expressway pass by. The Irish bus service, CIE, (*Córas Iompair Éireann*) I have also heard stands for 'Cram In Everybody.' I have no intention of cramming into any of their vehicles. The twenty miles to Ballyvaughan is eventually covered courtesy of two visitors from a country they call the 'U-Nighted States.' They come from St. Paul, Minnesota and are touring the west of Ireland. The driver, Harry, has a particular fascination for trying to guess other people's occupations and wants to know if I'm 'some kinda nut hitchin' round Ireland.' He goes through a range of jobs such as teacher, electrical engineer, fireman and playwright, before saying journalist.

They talk about the Gulf War. Harry says they postponed a holiday in Europe because of the war and weren't sure if it was safe to visit Ireland. He says Americans are not keen to travel when their country is at war and his brother even cancelled a planned trip to Hawaii.

In Ballyvaughan the man serving the warm restorative morning tea at the Tea Junction cafe says the summer has been extremely quiet so far. He believes the Gulf War undoubtedly deterred many people from coming to Ireland. But another problem was the bad press the town received following an oil slick just over a mile off the shoreline. The slick developed after a French fish factory ship ran aground on the coastline. The man says the harbour commissioners and local authorities managed to contain it. However there was concern from local fishermen preparing for the lobster season and from shellfish farmers who were worried about the effects of pollution in the bay.

'The slick was cleared up very quickly and was not as serious as many people imagined,' he says. 'But that sort of thing does a lot of damage to the image of a small place like this and takes some time to recover from.'

In the clear waters around Ballyvaughan Bay there is no apparent sign of any pollution. Two mute swans patrol the water's edge with five cygnets. Behind me a blanket of mist is moving in to cover Cappanawalla Mountain and quickly envelops the cottages at its foot.

A man standing outside one of the cottages tells me the oil slick was the fault of the media. He says it was a load of rubbish which, to a large extent, the press made up. He asks me what I'm doing. I tell him I'm a fireman who has decided to see Ireland at first hand.

He reckons my chances of getting a lift round Black Head and along the coast to Doolin are poor. The road from Ballyvaughan can be compared to the Cushendun to Ballycastle coastal road in north Antrim. It has little or no business traffic and the main users are tourists. Those on it this Tuesday morning are selfish, unkind and inhospitable. As they pass me I also call them a variety of other adjectives under my breath. For almost two hours I watch them drive past ignoring my erect thumb. Oddly enough most return within ten or fifteen minutes. The reason seems to be that after they've driven a few miles along the road to Black Head they discover visibility out to sea is so bad that it's not worth driving any further.

The coastline of Connemara, which has been obscured for over an hour, is now becoming visible with the disappearance of the clouds and emergence of the sun. The mountains slowly appear and the colours of the landscape come to life. It's the first place on my journey where I have appreciated the changing colour patterns of the sea, the pallor of the sky and the chiaroscuro of the countryside.

As I can't afford to spend the entire day studying the chameleon-like colour schemes of north Clare, I abandon the idea of the Black Head route. I walk back through Ballyvaughan and on to the Lisdoonvarna road for the inland alternative. Within a short time a commercial traveller, specializing in the drapery and millinery business, takes me in his estate car via Corkscrew Hill to Lisdoonvarna. From there another lift brings me the few miles to Doolin.

* * * * *

I'd been puzzled for some days. According to my map Doolin does not exist. I couldn't find it on any other map either. There is somewhere called Fisherstreet, and nearby another place called Roadford. Don Shannon, the man who picks me up at Lisdoonvarna, agrees that it is a geographical conundrum and leads to some confusion. He says Fisherstreet is the name of the place at the harbour, but the true Doolin is half a mile inland at Roadford where the post office is to be found.

'In reality though there are umpteen Doolins,' Don chortles. 'There's Roadford Doolin, Fisherstreet Doolin, Carnane Doolin and Boherbee Doolin. There's also Doolin Point, Lough Doolin, and sometimes there's even a Doolin ferry boat.'

When Don drops me off I'm not sure whether I'm actually in Doolin or Fisherstreet. The place consists of several pubs, a few shops and a plethora of youth hostels. Back-packers are everywhere – the one breed of people guaranteed to put off a more professional hitchhiker. It's four o'clock in the afternoon. After a thirst-quenching pint I decide it's time to move on to try to get around the Cliffs of Moher to Lahinch.

It's an uphill walk of a mile and a half on to the coastal road but the weight of my rucksack and the fact that I'm not feeling well combine to make it appear at least twice that distance. I come to a crossroads where the Homestead Foodstore and petrol station are carrying on a busy trade. Although I'm near the coast I have lost sight of the sea. All around is flat farmland with fields of Charolais and Limousin cattle. A common sandpiper arrives on the scene, and a magpie, intent on its business, struts across the road chattering to itself in an extrovert fashion. Most traffic is heading inland towards Ennistymon. The coastal route is not attracting many vehicles.

I resolve to sit it out, or at least stand it out. A black labrador relieves the ennui. Like me he is a car-chaser except he runs after them on four legs. He tires of this activity and presents me with an empty scrunched-up Coke can which he drops at my feet, looking up with sad expectant eyes. I kick it away and he rushes after it bringing it back to my feet. The game continues for a few minutes until a man in a van from Greenisle Foods interrupts the afternoon's fun. He thinks the dog is mine. As we drive off I look back at the dejected figure sitting alone at the roadside with the can in his mouth.

Patrick McDonagh is on his way to Ennis via Lahinch where he's making a business call. He talks about a controversy in the area over the proposed building of an interpretative centre at the foot of Mullaghmore Mountain several miles inland. There is said to be strong backing for the project which will be built in the heart of the Burren. But it has also caused much division. He says many of his friends attended meetings in schools and community halls venting their opposition to the plans. Patrick thinks it is not a bad idea provided it blends into the surrounding countryside, but he feels there is bound to be an ecological impact.

The proposal for the interpretative centre has stirred people into action. Many NIMBY (not in my back yard) types have come out of the closet. They've joined pressure groups, lobbied politicians, organized campaign meetings against the plans and written scores of letters to the provincial and national press.

Behind all the argument and debate though Patrick believes there is a deeper question. This centres on the whole point of mass tourism and the damage it does to the local environment.

'If you get bus loads of Americans, Germans or French walking in large numbers all over it then it can only cause damage to a sensitive area.

Tourism is increasing all the time and is growing each year with more and more people coming here.'

Patrick says the proposition of the action group opposing the plan is that there is no need for a centre when the real thing is there in any case. I argue that tourists are just ordinary visitors who probably want to learn something about the country and why shouldn't they have a centre where the flora and history of the area are explained to them in detail? Patrick partly agrees. He says another question, as yet unanswered, is how tastefully or thoughtfully the Office of Public Works will carry out the building and what the finished product will look like.

Before he drops me Patrick says most people don't realize that the centre is being built simply because money is coming from the European Community. The people campaigning for the building don't want to lose the opportunity of taking the money in case the Community changes its mind.

Lahinch has a deserted air. Along the beach front the shop selling whipped ices is boarded up, the elevated wooden lifeguard posts are empty and the Treasure Island amusement arcade might as well be closed for all the business going on inside. It could be any seaside resort in the middle of winter, but this is Ireland in the middle of June. The sea is a deep turquoise. Giant rollers break in long uneven lines over the beach. Three children throw sticks for their pet collie to chase and a couple of young boys practise skateboarding techniques along the footpath. Several courting couples sit in parked cars watching the fading sun.

I consider my options. It's getting late to strike out further south in Clare so I choose to stay put for the night in Lahinch. All day my cold has been deteriorating and I've developed a nasty cough. Several hot ports help heat up the body engine. A warm bed will, I hope, provide the cure I need. Tomorrow will be a new beginning.

* * * * *

The Clare sun is trying to rise but not with any great degree of enthusiasm. It certainly isn't giving much warmth. On Clare FM Radio the forecast warns of squally showers; winds may reach hurricane force and there may be thunder with the possibility of magnetic storms over parts of the British Isles.

I pull on an extra sweater and prepare for another bracing day of sea air. By ten o'clock the gales have already reached the coastal road from Lahinch to Milltown Malbay. Fast angry waves are breaking in and there is a loud crash of the surf.

With sufficient luck my hitchhiking today will take me along the Clare coast to Kilkee, over to Kilrush and down to Killimer for the car ferry into County Kerry. According to my reckoning I'm behind schedule and with the big Kerry peninsulas looming ahead I need to cover as much ground as possible. If I take the ferry I will avoid Limerick city and miss the northern part of the county which runs alongside the Shannon. It will also mean a considerable boost to my progress and hasten my arrival into County Kerry.

The drivers of the two cars which take me from Lahinch to Milltown Malbay and on to Quilty both advise me not to bother with Kilkee. They say there is nothing worth seeing and it is a quiet road. Even though I am behind schedule I prefer to take the road less travelled, but after forty minutes begin to doubt the wisdom of this. My difficulty is overcome with the arrival of a Toyota Corolla driven by Sean Meany, from Limerick. He is going to his holiday home in Kilkee.

There is a big tradition over the years, Sean says, of Limerick families holidaying in the town. This goes back to the early part of the last century when steam vessels operated each day between the city and Kilkee. A train ride brought holidaymakers the rest of the way.

'It's difficult to know,' he adds, 'exactly what makes Kilkee so attractive. It's a reasonably quiet place most of the year but during July and August the population grows from about fifteen hundred to nearly ten thousand. Kilkee can cater for everyone's image of a seaside resort, and is a safe place with a decent beach.'

Sean has been holidaying here since he was a young boy. He remembers the children barefoot sixty years ago when he first visited the area. The girls wore long skirts to their ankles and most people had no money. He worked for a firm of solicitors in Limerick before he retired. Sean and his wife now spend as much of the summer as they can at their holiday retreat near Kilkee. He says this area has some of the highest waves in Ireland, reaching between fifteen and twenty feet. Undoubtedly the ideal spot for my South African surfing friends.

Kilkee was the winner of the tidy towns competition in 1983 and has a neat appearance. Its crescent shaped beach, which lies at the end of a rocky inlet, is a windswept place. Judging by the lack of people along what is called 'the strandline' the season has not started yet. In the shops the bygone days of the resort are reflected in black and white picture postcards from the Lawrence collection which show Victorian ladies holding on to their hats overlooking the sea. In the West End of the town the nine-teenth century houses with their bay windows have survived the passing years and the influx of visitors. The town centre has an air of slight superiority over places like Lahinch and Doolin – or is it Roadford? – and has managed to keep plastic neon signs to a minimum.

Kilkee has close links with Kilrush, eight miles south-east. The man from Kameo Cakes who brings me there tells me Kilrush is much bigger and is becoming more popular recently with the opening of a new marina. The paint, in fact, is barely dry on the Shannon showpiece – the Kilrush Creek Marina. The manager, John Hehir, says they are open but have not held the official ceremony.

'The men in the mohair suits have not given it their blessing yet, but we are very busy and business is brisk,' he says.

The marina grew out of the western yacht club in Cappa. It was a disused harbour and is being developed into a dockside marina centre with shops, apartments and houses. There are also twelve acres for on-shore building which the developers hope will attract private investors. The eventual aim is to turn the project into a port-of-call for yachtsmen from throughout Europe and further afield. John says they've already had substantial foreign interest.

'What the Europeans most like about it is the proximity to the town,' he says. 'From the marina it takes just five minutes to walk into Kilrush and the French in particular like the idea of having the facilities of the town so close. Shannon airport is just an hour away by car so, strategically, we are well located.

'For the cruising yachtsman this is the ideal place. We are right beside the Shannon Estuary which is uncrowded and largely undeveloped and there are numerous bays and islands to explore off the west coast. We also offer the option of over a hundred miles of inland cruising on Lough Derg or the River Shannon itself.'

He says it is a sheltered marina with due west winds. They have one hundred and eighteen pontoons which will be floated into position, and two hundred and fifty berths will be able to accommodate all types of sailing craft when completed. In addition, John says, there will be a fully-equipped boatyard for servicing and repairing vessels with the long-term aim being to build boats.

Kilrush has been designated a heritage town by the tourist board and is to be promoted as a maritime/market town. The board wants to establish a chain of marinas or mooring facilities for visitors every thirty-five nautical miles along the coast from Wexford to the Shannon. The European Regional Development Fund has given the Kilrush project nearly two million pounds. Besides the building of a village of eighty houses there are also plans to revive the area's past with the restoration of a number of fishermen's cottages on the water front.

The town's seafaring tradition and maritime past is on view in the heritage centre. A display of maps, photographs and newspaper cuttings show the history which the area has enjoyed and looks back on the days of the steamers on the Shannon. Cuttings tell the story of how the song *Are Ye Right There Michael?* by Percy French landed him in court for slander about the West Clare Railway Line. Pictures show Paupers Quay which commemorates those who died in poor conditions during the first half of the nineteenth century. Another section looks at tragedies on the Shannon and shipwrecks at sea around an area known as the 'Reef of Grief.' Kilrush's maritime future is also featured with plans of the new marina.

Before leaving town I visit Houlihan's chemist shop for cough mixture to try to ease the sore throat and cough I've developed from over exposure to cold weather, wind, rain and too much talking.

From Killimer, the crossing on the MV *Shannon Heather*, which links the town with Tarbert across the estuary, is a smooth ten minute ride. Two businessmen – an English and a Belgian – pick me up in Kilrush and take me across in their BMW. They are on their way to a seminar in Killarney. Details are given on their car radio about a magnetic storm forecast over the country tonight. The announcer says communications and power lines could be disrupted and there may be a chance to see the *aurora borealis*.

For the next forty miles my north Kerry coastal route from Tarbert is peppered with towns of the Bally variety. From Ballylongford the road leads to Ballybunion, then runs through Ballyduff, Ballynaskreena and on to Ballyheige. A swift lift takes me from Tarbert to the first of them – Ballylongford. The area is rich productive farmland. A mournful herd of dairy cattle make their way past me on the road oblivious to what the Shannon Development people in their brochure call the '*tangible sense of history all around them.*'

The man who brings me to Ballybunion says it is not the place it was thirty or even forty years ago.

'To be honest it has totally gone to the dogs,' he observes. 'We don't seem to be able to attract the visitors and holiday makers that we did in days gone by. The place has really lived too long in the past and has not been able to throw off the 1950s image that many people have of it. They prefer going to south Kerry or Cork where there are more attractions. Over the years this place has become neglected. The only people who seem to keep coming back are the golfers.'

The town consists of a couple of streets, and a tight cluster of houses and hotels gathered around the harbour. Dimly lit pubs sit beside fast food outlets, amusement arcades and a casino that could indeed be *circa* 1950. I had thought of pushing on along the coast but the man who'd picked me up said after seven o'clock it would be a waste of time trying to get any further.

The sea front, with its rows of guest houses – each complete with a glass-fronted porch – has a timeless feel about it. The Anchorage B & B, overlooking the remains of the castle and the sea, seems as good a place as any from which to view the night sky. I am anticipating a spectacular evening with the possibility of taking some pictures of the Ballybunion 'son et lumière' night time display.

Ballybunion is named after the thirteenth century family, Bonyon. In the post office which also doubles as the tourist office, grocery shop and dispensing place for the all important tickets for the national weekly lottery, the postmaster tells me that Bonyon had nine daughters. One of them started going out with a son of a rival landowner. None of the daughters would tell their father which one it was, and according to legend, in his anger he drowned all nine at a spot which is known as the 'Nine Daughters' Blowhole.'

The postmaster says the main holiday rush will get underway soon. The big attraction is the twenty-first international bachelor festival which he says draws people from all over Ireland and abroad.

The beach at Ballybunion south has lost its blue flag award because of the removal of sand and gravel. The postmaster says a special prize was presented to the town by a coastal environment group for what they called the *'unending stamina, determination and investment in trying to halt the destruction of the beach by the licenced removal of material.'* Like the one at Roundstone in County Galway the beach here is of special interest. It is said to be of international geological and geomorphological importance. The Italians have obviously not heard about it yet.

In the Central Hotel on main street a *karaoke* night is in progress. A closer inspection reveals a crowd of perhaps fifty or sixty young girls screaming, smoking, swearing and occasionally singing. The Japanese invention to which amateurs singalong to a recorded backing is big business and is the main form of entertainment in many of the towns and villages I've visited.

The Beatles seem to be the most popular group for the *karaoke* fans in Ballybunion. Groups of girls at tables break into paroxysms of laughter, stub out their cigarettes and then pluck up the courage to push each other on to the stage. Four strapping Kerry women without a note in their combined heads take the stage to sing one of the worst renditions I've ever heard of *She Loves You.*

At one point the man introducing the acts runs outside in pursuit of a girl who has hurried off in embarrassment at being asked to perform *Hey Jude.* A trio of teenagers take the stage somewhat sheepishly at first but soon get into their rhythm for *Those Were The Days* and *Coal Miner's Daughter.* So great is their enthusiasm that the compère reminds them they're not supposed to eat the microphone. Spurred on by this a writhing duo step up to perform *The Locomotion* and follow it up with *I Will Survive*. I wasn't sure if my eardrums would. In the world of *karaoke*, enthusiasm does not unfortunately make up for lack of talent.

The word '*karaoke*,' I'm reliably informed by the man in charge of the machine, means 'empty orchestra.' He says the girls love it because anyone can join in. After two or three groups take the stage, he says, there is no stopping the rest.

'Carry-okay,' as he pronounces it, 'will become a big thing in Ireland over the next few years. It will be be part of the fabric of Irish life during the nineties and well into the next century,' he predicts. 'It improves pubs as it turns them into entertainment centres and somewhere people eagerly look forward to coming to.'

There is no doubting that *karaoke* is simple harmless fun, and certainly fills the pubs and hotels, but it's a sad reflection on the limited amount of real entertainment available in the Ballybunions of the nineties. By midnight I've had enough. With my ears buzzing I walk outside hoping to search out the activity in the night sky and the Kerry '*son et lumière*.' Sadly it is not to be. There are heavy showers though, and rumbles of distant thunder. Large black balls of cloud move swiftly eastwards through the night sky across the mouth of the Shannon. But the only sign of a sound and light show is the twinkle of Loop Head lighthouse on the south tip of County Clare and the continuing caterwauling coming from the girls singing and dancing to the *karaoke* machine in the Central Hotel.

SEARCHING FOR GOLDEN BACKS

Ballybunion to Glenbeigh

It's another dull morning; the sky is cloudy and everything is grey. From Ballybunion the road to Ballyduff leads off to the right while the main route out of town is the inland road to Tralee. After more than an hour of fruitless hitching I opt for the inland route through Listowel. A lift with a teacher covers the distance between Listowel and Tralee via the Six Crosses. He is on his way to Tralee to pick up a group of handicapped children for a trip in the country.

The signs at the edge of Tralee on the road to Dingle say the town is a sister city of Shawnee, in Kansas, and is twinned with Downpatrick in County Down. In Tralee it's time for my weekly visit to the launderette. After my clothes cleaning exercise I am determined to try to get the forty miles to Dingle by evening.

Seven roads radiate out from Tralee. The one I want leads along the northern side of the Dingle peninsula beside Tralee Bay over to Camp. The peninsula is the most northerly of Kerry's promontories that protrude into the Atlantic. My hitching spot affords a thrilling view of the lengthy range of the Slieve Mish Mountains, the eastern portion of which is obscured from view by cloud. The view is, unfortunately, ruined by a flock of seagulls circling around the town's dump. Not the best introduction to the Dingle peninsula which is regarded as one of County Kerry's major attractions. South Kerry has a different personality and history to the northern part of the county. The Kerry guide says the Dingle peninsula with its mountains, glacial valleys, lakes, islands, strands and vast sand hills is a landscape of antiquity.

Pat Laffan, the area manager of a company selling insurance and pension schemes to farmers, is going as far as Stradbally which will bring me close to the Connor Pass. We share an interest in the wild flowers. Pat makes no claims to be an expert but when we get to Mattie Moloney's Bar at Stradbally we meet someone who is. Michael John O'Shea is a horticulturist who is helping in the landscaping and development of a golf course on the shores of Lough Gill beside Castlegregory. He brings me down a minor road to the shore front at Tralee Bay and introduces me to an unsurpassed selection of wild flowers, many of which I've never seen before.

Inside the space of sixty minutes we find ragged robin with its narrow red leaves growing in abundance around the shores of the lough. We see long-leaved early purple orchids, bulbous buttercups, field pansies or heartsease (which have small cream flowers), and which Michael says is sometimes referred to as viola tricolor, and marsh marigold which is a perennial of the buttercup family and is also called kingcup. It's a flower I believe I last heard of while on a nature study walk at primary school. We come across bird's foot trefoil, yellow rattle and sea holly with its pale blue head which grows widely around the coast and on sand. Michael is getting into his stride and as we continue our fast-paced walk we discover black medick, bog bean which was used at one time by country people as a remedy for boils, bog mint, hare's foot clover and the rare shrubby cinquefoil.

Michael then switches tack from flora to fauna and tells me about a small creature that inhabits the area: the natterjack toad. The toads are dying out in the British Isles and this is the only place in Ireland where they are found. He says they are still breeding in some parts of England and southern Scotland, but are extinct in Wales. Over eighty per cent of their breeding sites have been lost this century. Their habitat at Castlegregory is underneath stones and rocks, and buried deep into the sand dunes. Michael quarters the ground like a bloodhound in his quest for the natterjack. He turns over ten or twelve stones and searches clumps of grass before we uncover our first toad. One quickly leads to another and soon scores of the small olive green animals are scurrying around through the grass and dunes looking for hiding places. Michael sets one in the palm of his hand. He points out the distinctive yellow stripe from the head along the centre of the back. They used to be called golden backs, he tells me, and were commonly known as running toads, because of the fact that they run rather than hop. He says this means they are able to forage more efficiently for food than the common toad, the only other toad native to the British Isles. The natterjacks search for insects, worms and any grubs they can find.

Michael says the toads like this site with its shallow ponds and sandy soils where they burrow easily. Their numbers have now grown to several hundred and they are a protected species. After darkness, during the calm nights in May, they congregate in large numbers at the edge of the ponds and spend several hours building into a croaking crescendo. He says when they come out of their daytime hiding places at dusk they raise their heads, crank their vocal cords into action and begin their chorus. The calls are intended to drive off other males as well as attract females. Michael says it's quite a striking sight and sound. The call lasts for only a second, but on warm still nights it can be heard over a mile away. Listening to a knot of toads echoing around the fields and lakes of Kerry sounds an idyllic way of spending an evening. I make a note to return to the area in May and check their amphibian love songs for myself.

There were fears that the natterjack would die out in the area because of the positioning of a hole at the golf links at Castlegregory. It would have gone through their breeding grounds, but Michael explains they managed to reach a compromise that avoided encroaching on the toads' habitat and part of the course is now a nature reserve. From October onwards, when the nights start getting cooler, the toads hibernate and emerge from their burrows the following April when the weather has warmed up. As we part company he says many people are amazed that toads should be found on a golf course, but he offers the suggestion that if golfers can have eagles and birdies, then why not toads?

I thank Michael for his instructive and entertaining tour. The afternoon has been most educational but it has seriously hindered my attempt to reach Dingle; it is now approaching seven o'clock. I make my way back up to the main road at Stradbally in search of a lift over the Connor Pass. The traffic has all but dried up. My company at the start of what turns out to be a seventy minute wait are a couple of stonechats sitting at the opposite end of the wall of a bridge. They take a brief interest in me. One jumps down and chases a fly which manages to escape. It then makes a feeble attempt to grab another insect but with no success. I try to catch a couple of passing motorists but also with no success.

Most cars seem to be going back towards Camp. I toy with the idea of going there and cutting inland through Anascaul to get over to Dingle. However, perseverance pays off again and shortly after eight, a couple holidaying from London, bring me the ten miles across the precipitous Connor Pass. We stop to admire the views. On our right Brandon Peak sticks up into the clear night air and behind it rises Brandon Mountain, Ireland's second highest peak, standing at three thousand one hundred and twenty-seven feet.

In Dingle I check into the Harbour View B & B which, given the amount of building work going on outside, should be more aptly named 'Stone Block' or 'JCB view.' The fish in Greany's restaurant is far and away the best I've had so far on the trip. That, of course, would not be difficult as most of the food has been mediocre. It is a marvellously unpretentious cafe where the fresh north shore deep fried haddock comes on fish shaped glass plates. The food is so good that I even forgive the management for misspelling Ballygowan. It appears under the listings for beverages as 'Ballygown.' The American waitress tells two American girls that the ice cream in Ireland is better than anything served up in New Jersey, or for that matter anywhere in the States. The owner, John Greany, says in 1965 his was the only restaurant in Dingle. Over the years the numbers gradually increased and there are now more than twenty, and perhaps as many as forty establishments serving food, if you count pubs.

The main focus of attention in Dingle has centred on plans to build two marinas. Work has already begun on one at the harbour with which most people seem to be happy. But there is intense opposition to a plan by the owners of the Skellig Hotel to build a marina at their site.

John says there is a crying need to attract jobs to the town. He talks about the controversial plans for the Dingle marina developments. Most people, he believes, are keen enough to have the harbour development, but not the one at the Skellig Hotel. The Skellig wants twenty-three acres of foreshore land to build chalets, condominiums and cottages and he feels it would destroy the look of the harbour marina. 'People need to care about the topography and look of the countryside as well as its aesthetic appeal,' he says.

John reckons that twenty years from now Dingle could be what he calls a 'hell on earth' the same as the south of France or south of Spain with no room to move around in. As it is, in the busy season Dingle's streets can't cope with the number of tourists.

'If you go for a tour around Slea Head you will see what I mean. Holiday homes and cottages are being built all over the place with no thought for planning controls or restrictions.'

For several weeks in May more than fifty witnesses, vigorously cross-examined by lawyers, were called to give evidence at a public inquiry into the private Skellig development. It was held by the Department of the Marine. Many reasons were outlined by the objectors who were led by Dingle Chamber of Commerce. They claimed, amongst other things, the development would pose a navigational hazard, damage the wildlife, cause pollution, create a satellite town within Dingle, and would mean giving away twenty-three acres of prime public land which would cause erosion to the foreshore. Some of the evidence to the inquiry was given in Irish and was translated by an interpreter. One witness, who said he was a writer, poet, singer and musician, told the inquiry he was representing the hard working people who pay a lot of tax. He said he had a hump on his back from paying so much tax.

Feelings in Dingle run deep against the Skellig development. The Chamber of Commerce has set up a harbour defence fund and many shops and pubs display large hand painted signs in windows which say:

NOT ONE INCH OF DINGLE FORESHORE SHOULD BE GIVEN TO THE SKELLIG HOTEL

SOS: SAVE OUR SHORE

THOU SHALT HAVE NO FALSE MARINA BEFORE ME

The directors of the Skellig Hotel told the inquiry the development would bring a further two and half million pounds into the town each year and would create twenty-five jobs. At the hotel itself Sean Clusky, the manager, tells me he is happy with the plans. He sees the whole concept as a tremendous prospect which, along with the Kilrush marina, will link up the whole of the west coast of Ireland.

'People have no objections to having two pubs, two hotels or two restaurants, so why should we not have two marinas?' he asks. He says their first plan is for a marina and they have not yet thought out the full development of the apartments at this stage. That will come much later. Sean is aware of the strength of opposition to the Skellig plans, but he says the government supports the hotel development and believes it is a good idea.

The landlady in the misnamed Harbour View, Anne Griffin, is perplexed. She says it is difficult to know what to make of it all.

'We used to have a great view of the harbour with the water coming up to the wall on the other side of the road. Now as you can see it is just a pile of stones. They are building a breakwater and have promised us it will look good when it is finished. At the start I was very much against the idea, but when I gave it some consideration I couldn't really see what harm there would be in building two marinas. If they've got firm orders for berths and the boats want to come in then that means business for the whole town, and there must be sufficient people who will want to use them.'

* * * * *

The next morning it's too wet to start hitching so I spend an hour or two around the town. In *An Café Liteartha* bookshop a cup of hot coffee relieves the morning gloom. The main story of the week in *The Kerryman* newspaper is about how killer whales stalked Dingle's dolphin, Fungie – the big tourist attraction.

It says the dolphin had a narrow escape from death when a school of nine killer whales stalked him in the mouth of the harbour. The whales, known as *Orcas*, are the fiercest predators in the ocean. A spokesman from the Department of Marine is quoted as saying their bite is a diameter of over three feet which enables them to chop a full grown dolphin in half. Fungie, it appears, moved with incredible speed when the whales came in and sheltered in Sladeen. The whales are the most sophisticated hunters in the sea and the dolphin would have been easy prey for them. The news of Fungie's escape from the clutches of death comes at the same time as the government announced that all Irish seas are to be whale and dolphin sanctuaries. Fungie was first sighted in 1984. He is now so well known that a book about his life story featuring pictures and drawings is one of the best sellers in Dingle. The existence of this sea-creature is obviously vital to the economy of the town.

Much as I would like to remain inside the bookshop I know it is time for the road. Under the relative dryness of the roof of Moran's garage I wait for a lift to take me along the south side of the peninsula through Anascaul, Castlemaine and with any luck, start my circuit of the Iveragh peninsula, or as it's more commonly known, the Ring of Kerry.

A grey Rolls Royce Silver Shadow whooshes past and throws up a spray. The opulence and money associated with the town is further demonstrated when two Jaguars and a red Porsche drive past. Then one of Dingle's best known restaurateurs, John Doyle, stops to fill his Mercedes with petrol and enquires if I would like a lift. He doesn't have to ask twice. He is going to Tralee with his son and says he will take me as far as Anascaul.

John is interested in the marina plans and says one of the most important matters which has been overlooked is the visual aspect.

'We don't want an urban sprawl and an unsightly mess left by the developers,' he says. 'I went to Torremolinis in 1957. It was my first visit to what was then a pretty coastal village – but now look at it! It's pathetic; a terrible place, all monstrous tower blocks and concrete.

'You have to remember that in Dingle's case the raw sewage is going into the harbour where the development will be. If they build these apartments that will mean three hundred more toilets, and you can imagine the environmental hazards of that. For me though the visual appeal is most important. Ireland is a wild, rugged, beautiful country and I don't want to see it being despoiled by huge, ill-planned buildings.'

John drops me in the centre of Anascaul. A short lift brings me the few miles over to Inch with its four mile long beach. On the white gable wall of a closed up shop a local scribe has paraphrased Robert Frost's *Stopping By Woods On A Snowy Evening*:

Dear Inch, must I leave you
I have promises to keep,
Perhaps miles to go
To my last sleep.

I take refuge from the rain in a derelict hayshed. It has a leaking corrugated iron roof, but nevertheless keeps me dry. Across the bay the mountains of the Ring of Kerry are covered in cloud. A couple of herring gulls and the steady raindrops provide the only noise and the only life. There are no human voices in this delectable place.

The first car to come along stops. During the run to Castlemaine Michael O'Sullivan says he is interested in the political situation in the north. I tell him I find most people I have met on my trip don't want to bring up the subject. He says he would not wish to take his family into Northern Ireland because it would be too much hassle. 'I would not cross that border, even if you paid me,' he asserts. I tell him it's not as dangerous as most outsiders believe.

I'm dropped in Castlemaine and within a few minutes I've travelled the six miles to Killorglin to begin the one hundred mile circuit of the Ring of Kerry, which is said to be the busiest tourist route in Ireland. It's now three-thirty so I will have difficulty in completing the full trip today, but hope to at least make some inroads. My best chance, I feel, lies with a visitor as it is considered *de rigueur* for every self-respecting holidaymaker in Ireland to tour the peninsula. A leaflet from the tourist office in Killorglin describes the Iveragh peninsula as '*a continuous delight varying a hundred times in a hundred miles.*'

In a secondhand bookshop in Tralee I'd bought an old guide to the area dating from the 1930s. Sitting on a wall opposite Jacko Foley and Sons, Mace Convenience Express on the road to Glenbeigh, I note from its thin faded pages, not only how prices have dramatically changed, but also how services have slipped. The inclusive tariff for a week at the Imperial Hotel in Killarney in those days was sixty-three shillings. The International weekly rate was ninety shillings and porters in uniform met all trains. Today the equivalent of ninety shillings wouldn't even buy you a couple of drinks at the bar of the International. And sixty years on, a week there would set you back two hundred and eighty pounds.

From my book I see that this region, perhaps more than any other, has been the most written about in Ireland. It has, in some respects, become hackneyed. Nineteenth century romantic writers such as Wordsworth, Tennyson, Macaulay and Thackeray visited the lakes of Killarney and waxed lyrical about them. Wordsworth called it the most beautiful spot in the British Isles; Sir David Wilkie likened it to a Hibernian Switzerland and Queen Victoria described Killarney as '*Fairyland*.'

I've always been fond of old guidebooks and travel guides. I find them excellent travel companions and delightful to read on location. In her book called *Travels*, the writer Jan Morris says half the pleasures of old guidebooks are physical. She writes:

> *I love them as objects. It is only partly in their words; the rest is embodied in their smell of age and foreign ink, the suggestion of salt-spray on their bindings, the spindly signatures of their previous owners, or the faded pink Ticket of Admittance, tucked still within the museum itinerary, which, like a madeleine dipped in tea, can evoke so miraculously other times in distant places.*

(Morris, Jan. *Travels*, London. 1976).

An hour and a half passes. I've still made no progress to my distant destination, Glenbeigh. Most of the traffic passing me this Friday afternoon seems to be local. Spots of rain start to fall again. They have that threatening look of turning into something much heavier.

As ever determination and dedication pays off, and even though my lift when it comes is in a vehicle that looks as if it past its prime about twenty years ago I am happy to take it. I've watched customers come and go all afternoon at Jacko Foley's and am anxious for something more stimulating than seeing people buying petrol and bread. Pat O'Shea drives a beaten up Datsun Stanza. He is a heavily built red-faced man whose breath smells of whiskey. Within half a minute the passenger door flies open. Pat tells me I must hold it together with a piece of twine which is attached to the inside handle and which then ties round the handbrake. Most other switches and knobs on the dashboard are also held together with bits of string, sellotape or clips. In fact it seems something of an engineering triumph that it's even on the road. A loud grinding noise comes from the gearbox and Pat has difficulty engaging third gear. There is also a problem with the steering. He holds the wheel firmly but it doesn't seem to affect the direction of the wheels and the car gently slides from one side of the road to the other. If this vehicle was in Australia they would call it a Holden, because it's holdin' together.

Pat has had some bad luck with it. 'It was a terrible mishtake to buy this car in the first place,' he says. 'I've had her nearly five yearsh and she's given me nothin' but trouble for most of that time. And mind you I'm not very hard on her.'

Glenbeigh is journey's end with Pat. I step out into a village surrounded by mountains where the rain has now well and truly turned into a downpour. I stand with my back to birch trees and six-foot hedges of fuchsias and holly. After thirty minutes I reckon I've had enough for one day and make my way back through the village to check in to the Glenbeigh Hotel. Weary, wet and tired I've decided to go upmarket for the night as I'm not in the mood for rehearsing the details of my trip to another landlady in a guest house. The Glenbeigh Hotel has many attractions. It is relatively cheap and comfortable. It is an establishment full of warm old fashioned charm. Admittedly it doesn't have porters in uniform, but it does have plush sofas, soft chairs and, more importantly, heat. Turf fires blaze in the lounge, bar and dining room. In the lobby behind the reception desk a large polished mahogany cabinet with a sign across the top says '*Dispensing Department.*' Up the creaking stairs the bedrooms, with their solid furniture, have a comforting and reassuring appearance.

I seem to be the only guest in the hotel. After eating alone in a large music-free dining room, surrounded by six waiters and waitresses, I settle down with a nightcap in front of the fire in the hotel bar. It's the perfect end to a lousy day. The bar is a favourite spot for farmers. Sparks leap out of the fire on to a brown rug lying over the carpet. The capriciousness of the weather is the main topic of discussion. All along the coast on my journey so far this has been the case. And for the people of Glenbeigh, like so many others in the towns and villages I've passed through, it is not just a topic to bridge the conversational gap, but something which affects and shapes their livelihood and day to day existence.

I strike up an alliance with a farmer wearing a plum coloured jacket. He tells me – as if I need any confirmation – the past two weeks have been the wettest start to June he can remember. He gives me some more grounds for dissatisfaction. 'You should have been here in May,' he says cheerily. 'We had three weeks of non-stop sunshine. In fact there was actually a drought in some parts. We hardly saw any sign of rain for the whole month.'

I have heard this line, or something similar, more than twenty times since leaving Belfast. It seems all the way along the west coast on my anticlockwise journey I've been following the driest and hottest spell of weather in recent Irish history. My friend is warming to his theme. 'Oh, yerra, to be honest with you it was really too hot in May. But then people are never bloody well satisfied, are they? It's either too hot, too cold, too wet or too dry and of course 'tis true what they say that the farmers are always complaining.'

I nod my head and quote to him the famous quip attributed to 'Uncle Mark':

Everybody talks about the weather but nobody does anything about it.

The farmer gives me a crooked grin. I bid him goodnight and retire to my comfortable room with the Kerry guide by my bedside. I see that for their part the tourist board believe poor weather should not be seen in any negative respect. It should in fact be regarded as a positive factor. The guide claims the weather is an integral part of the beauty of the county and the visitor must learn to roll with it:

> *Heavy intermittent rain need not be a deterrent and often enhances the view in the peninsulas. Heavy continuous rain can be magnificent in the mountains: to drive through Ballaghabeama on a really bad day is an experience to remember. A calm drizzle gives delightful effects along the Killarney lakes . . .*

And so it goes on. It is an experience I feel I can happily miss. You have to admire the writing talent and sheer audacity of people who work for the tourist board. With the rain beating down ever harder on the hotel roof I reflect on another epigram from 'Uncle Mark' who wrote of a summer he'd once had in California:

> *The coldest winter I ever spent was a summer in San Francisco.*

DOWN TO THE MEMBRANE

Glenbeigh to Schull

I hit the road early and take stock of the trip. It is day fifteen – the halfway stage. I have so far clocked up eight hundred miles. I now want to tackle the Ring of Kerry and then make some headway on the Beara peninsula.

By nine-thirty good fortune favours me in the form of Sean Bric. He is travelling to Cahersiveen, or as he calls it 'Kayhursauveen' to check on his suckler cows. Sean is from Tralee and has lived in the area all his life. He knows the surrounding countryside well and he has climbed most of the mountains, including Carrauntoohil, the highest peak in Ireland.

Sean yawns every few minutes. I'm not sure if my presence is boring him or if he is just tired, but he doesn't seem to want to talk. Perhaps it's too early in the day. I sit back and admire the scenery. Dealing with suckler cows, I imagine, must breed a certain taciturnity. We pass signs on the road pointing to the Kerry Way which Sean says will eventually provide a circuit of the peninsula. He says The Way consists of pads, butter roads, old railway tracks, and routes of early Christian settlements. The clouds have not yet lifted from most of the inland peaks. When we get to Cahersiveen Sean says he'll be going on in about half an hour's time to Castlecove, twenty miles further round the ring. If I'm still on the road he'll pick me up again.

Cahersiveen is the archetypal Irish town with a long meandering main street made up of shops and pubs. I buy a newspaper and think about having a coffee, but rather than miss the onward chance of a lift with Sean I walk to the edge of town and wait for the appearance of his Toyota at the side of the road, not really making an effort to hitch other vehicles.

The Kerry guide says Cahersiveen grew up at the beginning of the nineteenth century. It has two notable buildings. One is the O'Connell memorial church to honour the centenary of Daniel O'Connell's birth. The other is the ruins of a police barracks, intended, it is said, for the north-west frontier. The plans however were mixed up. In the War of Independence the building was burnt down.

Before I've time to explore the town's architectural heritage Sean reappears. From Cahersiveen we swing south down to Waterville where he says the holiday firm Club Med have opened a new complex. Because of the wet weather and dampness associated with Kerry it has become known to local people as 'Club Mud.' Sean's yawn rate has decreased. As we continue over the Coomakesta Pass he points out the Skellig Islands lying out in the Atlantic. He regularly drives along this road and says it has become something of a trial, especially during the busy summer months when it is choked with tourist coaches.

Sean drops me at Castlecove, near Derrynane harbour. It has been one of my longest morning lifts so far. The time is eleven o'clock and I've already covered more than fifty miles. The problem now is that I am deposited on an open country road and consequently it will be more difficult attracting traffic to stop to take me the ten miles to Sneem.

After an hour hanging around ditches I walk for a mile or so until the almost mandatory raindrops – the familiar Kerry drizzle so beloved by the tourist board – start to fall. All this time my cold has been steadily deteriorating and the medicine I bought in Kilrush is finished without producing the desired effect of clearing up my cough. I resolve to visit another chemist's shop when I get to Sneem.

My map shows Sneem as having a peaceful panda and a metal tree. This seems as good a reason as any to check the place over. The guidebook says the village is two hundred years old. The name Sneem means '*knot*' and it has therefore become known as the knot in the Ring of Kerry. A couple from Austria take me in the back of their campervan the short distance into the village which is bursting with tour coaches. A bridge, where the Sneem river and two tributaries meet, separates the village in two.

The metal tree is actually a stainless steel sculpture presented by President Chaim Herzog of Israel in 1985 as a tribute to the memory of a former President of State. The peaceful panda, it turns out, is a white marble panda on a rock in a walled enclosure at the corner of Quay Road. It was built in 1986 as a symbol of the friendship between Ireland and China which was promoted by the former Irish President, Cearbhall O'Dalaigh who retired to live in the village.

Sneem, for some reason, has over the years attracted a large number of retired people. In the village museum one wall is devoted to pen pictures of the great and good who've connections with the place. They include

Charles de Gaulle (he who said losing the battle is not losing the war), the architect, Michael Scott, Fr. Michael Walshe, who was the legendary Fr. O'Flynn of the ballad by Alfred Perceval Graves (the father of Robert Graves), the playwright George Bernard Shaw and last, but not least, Steve Casey 'The Crusher,' the world heavyweight all-in wrestling champion, from 1939 to 1948 who was born in the village.

Burke's Medical Hall looks as if it might be the type of place to provide a remedy for my deep-seated cough. The owner, Cyril Burke, is a man of immediate friendliness. However he gives me a gentle rebuke when I impart the details of my trip. He ponders for a moment over the best medicine for me and concludes that I need what he calls a 'Sneem Special.' It is certain, he declares, to drive away the cough.

'What you must do is get through the throat and down to the membrane,' he says. He disappears for a few minutes and returns with his very own concoction which he hands over to me. 'Take half a teaspoon of that today every two hours, and tomorrow take the same dosage every five hours.'

Cyril tells me his potion should have a bit of a kick to it but will be easy to swallow.

'This is one of the older type of cures and will certainly clear your chest during the day. But it will also clear up that harsh cough. A lot of the old cures were good but many were absolutely hopeless. The old chemists worked on what they saw. They asked people what they were suffering from and worked out a bottle of stuff according to that. The standard bottles of medicine you get nowadays don't really treat the individual problems. It's all instant and pre-packaged but what people don't realize is that commonsense will treat most conditions.' Cyril gives me a wag of his finger and urges me not to stand in the rain too long. 'If you are on the road out in cold weather then you need a little bit of help, but you must remember that your body cures yourself. Treat it with a little respect and everything will be all right.'

Cyril's 'Sneem Special' contains *sodium citrate, diphenhydramine, ammonium chloride* and menthol. For all I know though he could have thrown into it some of the natural cod liver oil, epsom salts, a-tak-a-rat, touch-me-not fly repellent or louse powder all sitting on the shelves of his shop. Still, he has been in business for forty years and I reckon he must be familiar with his dispensing duties. He reminds me again that I must, at all costs, get down to the membrane. 'That is crucial to getting rid of the cold, and you should never forget it at any time.'

Cyril talks about life in Sneem. He says the main appeal of the place for people who come to live in it, is that they rarely have any serious crime in the area.

'It is really a very small place and nobody bothers much about anybody else. People come for the peace and quietness and for the views. And the most important thing is they know when they come here they will be left alone. Sneem has not yet caught up with the modern type of vandalism found in other parts of the country. People here are friends and rivals. In other towns they are rivals watching one another and will not be able to lend a hand to their neighbours, but that is not the case here. We've a population of about seven hundred and everyone knows everyone else.'

Cyril's views about crime ring true. On the street the only visible sign of any misdemeanour is on a notice board in the North Square where information is being sought about a stolen flag.

Sneem is a village full of flower boxes with roses and geraniums. It is an agreeable little place but no longer a secret. From my hilly vantage point on the road to Kenmare I watch coach party after coach party come and go. Fortunately there are no beaches nearby so most people pass through after taking pictures of the mountains from the bridge. Most head round the ring or turn back along the inland road to Killarney. The village could well be set in the Rockies with its mountains, clear air, church spires and wide-bodied coaches. One passes me with the initials SAGA written across the front window in large letters. The company operates holidays for older people and it is said the firm's initials stand for 'Send All Grannies Away.'

After a fifty minute spell at this spot I begin to wonder if I will make it into the Beara peninsula. Perhaps I should stop overnight at Kenmare, if I ever get there, and start afresh in the morning. I take a couple of swigs of the 'Sneem Special' and before I've time to replace the cap a young German pulls up in a Vauxhall Nova.

My lift, with Wolfgang who comes from Erkrath, near Dusseldorf, is the magical transformation in my luck that I've been waiting for. He says he is on a tour of the youth hostelries of Ireland and has hired a car for four days. He has done some hitching himself and sympathizes with lone figures standing at the roadside. Wolfgang's girlfriend was to have come with him but broke her arm before leaving. He is undecided as to where to go for the evening and when I tell him I wish to get to Castletownbere he says that is a perfect suggestion. It is an eighty mile drive through Kenmare, into the Beara peninsula, and over the Healy Pass to Castletown. Signs say the Pass is unsafe for horse caravans. Along what Wolfgang calls 'the sigsag raout' there are viewing points for admiring the scenery.

We make our way along a tortuous route with bare mountains on either side and stop at the top to see the breathtaking mass of the Kerry peaks. The sun has come out to reveal the wavy line of the two thousand feet Caha Mountains. On the other side the Slieve Miskish Mountains stretch off into the distance. County Kerry shares the Beara peninsula with County Cork and the mountains straddle the county border. It is a jigsaw of rivers, bogland, small islets, rocks and mountains. There is a fine view north to the Iveragh peninsula where the high peaks glow purple and brown. The Caha Mountains get their name from the Irish word *ceatha*, 'showers.' This afternoon they've stayed away and I'm enjoying the best view of the mountain ranges I've had anywhere. Immediately below us from our viewing point is Glanmore Lake and beside it a ring fort which looks almost complete. From here the road drops down steeply in twisty fashion until we get to Adrigole where it is a ten mile run over to Castletown. It is eight o'clock by the time we reach the fishing port. I arrange to meet Wolfgang later to buy him a drink in the Old Irish Pub.

The woman running the guest house I've chosen – a bungalow on the edge of town – says they don't get too many tourists in the area because there is a shortage of accommodation. Castletown, she says, is not geared to cope with a large influx of visitors as there is only one hotel. The tourist office is housed in a caravan in the centre of the main street. A notice on the window says Beara is for the discerning visitor who wants to get away from everything and find peace and tranquillity. By this they mean avoiding the coach tours and throngs of people along the Ring of Kerry. It describes Beara as '*an area of untamed wildness and unspoiled beauty.*'

Over a couple of drinks Wolfgang tells me of the places he has visited on his holiday. He liked the Giant's Causeway in County Antrim but did not like Donegal as there were 'too many stones in it,' especially on Errigal. He was particularly keen on Galway and thought Connemara was 'vair goot.'

The pub is gearing up for a Saturday night music session. It is a relief to find the *karaoke* machine has not percolated this far west in County Cork. The only evidence of any visitors is a party of four from Dublin who arrive at eleven o'clock and complain about the four and a half hour drive to get to the town. The Old Irish Pub is a traditional bar. Small, dark and with a low ceiling it is a place where such gems as *The Black Velvet Band, The Fields of Athenry* and *From Clare to Here* are played on a squeeze box, fiddle and penny whistle with tremendous zest and enthusiasm. Wolfgang laps it all up. He has not heard such lively music since leaving the Irish pubs of Dusseldorf.

* * * * *

I wake up refreshed after my first night in what is known locally as the 'independent state of west Cork.' The 'Sneem Special' appears to have done the trick as my throat feels much better. Castletownbere is stretch-

ing slowly awake like a cat. At nine o'clock the Sunday papers lie un-
opened in bundles on the ground at the front of Breen's lobster bar and
newsagency. On my way through the town to the Adrigole Road the
streets are deserted except for a few parked cars.

To say the flow of traffic out of Castletown on the Sunday morning of
my visit is quiet, is probably the understatement of the trip. Four vehicles
pass me in the first half hour. They are driven by farmers towing metal
canisters containing milk. I like watching towns come awake; just as well
as it is something I have become familiar with in recent weeks. At least it
is a dry morning which encourages a woman further along from me at
Blackrock Terrace to come out with a chair, clean the windows, polish the
knocker on her door and scrub the doorstep.

I peruse the map. I want to get along the south coast of the Beara
peninsula to Glengarriff and, assuming I can find a driver willing to take
me, head through Bantry into the Mizen peninsula. Three Spanish fishermen walk past giving me a wary look. A small white yacht sails into the
harbour and a couple of boats putter here and there. I try my luck for
another half hour. I don't even have the consolation of the Sunday papers
to provide me with my morning news fix as Breen's is still locked up.

Most cars are taking the road to Killarney where Cork are playing Kerry
in the Munster gaelic football semi-final. Sixty thousand people are
expected to attend. By this time yesterday I'd covered fifty miles. Today,
nothing, and no prospect of anything. Such are the vicissitudes of hitchhiking. Life on the road though has shown me that just when desperation
starts to creep in, a change in fortunes usually comes about.

A white transit van pulls up ten yards ahead of me. Colum Cronin is a
country music singer, famed he claims, 'far and wide throughout west
Cork.' He has spent the night on Bere Island where he provided the
entertainment at a social gathering for members of the civil defence
forces. He describes it as a sort of weekend knees up in a big gymnasium.

Colum has been on the local music scene for twenty years and has
produced several cassettes. He mainly plays at private functions such as
weddings and parties, but also sings in lounge bars to keep his name in the
public mind. He says he has no ambitions to become known countrywide
and is happy with his small patch covering west Cork. He runs his own
recording studio and describes himself as a one-man band.

'I play the guitar with expanders and synthesizers and record all my own
stuff,' he says. 'But as well as that I am also the distributing, marketing and
publicity manager. The country music scene is in a fairly poor state at the
moment due to the recession. The big bands have fragmented because of
the costs involved and many have turned into smaller groups with just two
or three performers. It makes for more competition and for price cutting to

get the jobs. For example, the pub scene is reasonably healthy, but if a musician agrees to a price of say fifty pounds for playing in a pub for the night and if he fills that place ten times over he won't get paid anything extra for drawing the crowds. I think that is grossly unfair, but that is the way the system works.'

Colum's enthusiasm for the area is obvious. He loves playing the local halls because there is such a rapport with the audience and he says there is a tremendous community spirit in places such as Adrigole or Castletown.

'The big thing at the moment in west Cork is the revival of the *ceilidh*. People are flocking in their hundreds to set dancing classes all over the area throughout the winter and many young people are taking part which is great to see. At the parties I attend nowadays I have to play polka sets which was unheard of in the villages here a few years ago.'

Colum declares the *karaoke* machine a rip off and says people are making fools of themselves dancing to it. He suggests it won't last and thinks it will be a passing craze as people come to appreciate live music again.

We pass through Glengarriff. Several distinguished looking hotels sit at the harbour and the mountains provide a backdrop. 'This sort of country-side and landscape is inspirational for musicians and writers,' says Colum. On his cassette machine he plays a sample of his music. *Welcome to west Cork* is one of his best known numbers:

> *Come friends with me and I'll let you see*
> *The most beautiful sights in our country*
> *We'll head down to west Cork in the south of our Isle*
> *And the beauty and charm there will soon make you smile*
> *See the high rocky mountains and the far-reaching glens*
> *The long sandy beaches, the lakes and hills*
> *You may travel the world, but I'm sure you'll agree,*
> *The beauty of west Cork you never will see.*

I take my leave of Cronin the west Cork Crooner who, as well as brightening up my day, has transported me the thirty-five miles to Bantry.

* * * * *

Toasted sandwiches and drinks are being served in the Anchor Bar where I meet a like-minded spirit. Bill O'Donnell, the owner, is in his sixties. A newspaper cutting on the wall from the *London Evening News*, dated August the 14th 1958, tells of his exploits when he hitchhiked eight thousand miles around the world over the course of six years. He says he had a serious case of wanderlust in his youth. It was a travel bug which reached global proportions. He set off in the early fifties with seventy pounds in his pocket and worked his way through many countries.

'In Afghanistan there were only two main roads in the whole country,' he recalls. 'The worst road in the world at that time was the one hundred and sixty miles between Farah and Herat.' Two weeks before Bill arrived there the river valleys had flooded and parts of the road were impassable. The only way to cross was by camel.

'The conditions were terrible. I nearly froze to death on the mountain passes wearing only a shirt and shorts. It took me more than twenty hours to get to Herat and when I finally arrived they had to thaw me out in front of a fire.'

Bill travelled around the Far East, hitching and then working when he ran out of money.

'I went from truck depot to truck depot and quite honestly my Irish passport was an open sesame. It was a marvellous experience from the educational point of view. You have to remember there wasn't much in Ireland in those days. For example there was no television. I lived for a period in each country I visited and loved soaking up different cultures and meeting people. And I found the best way of doing that was hitchhiking.'

On his travels Bill also managed to pick up a wife. He met his wife, Tooey, in Rarotonga in the Cook Islands of the South Pacific and he admits that he has been very lucky. She now works with him in Bantry behind the bar. He is interested in the minutiae of my trip and says if he wasn't confined to managing the bar he would grab his rucksack and come with me.

'I love hitching. For me, until the grave, there will always be the magic of getting out on the open road and being a free spirit. The fun is in jumping into a car with a stranger, and not knowing where you will be by the end of the day.' Bill laughs. 'If you told me I had to go to Dublin tomorrow morning and if I was in no particular hurry then the only way I would go would be on the thumb. You meet such a remarkable span of people and it is so fascinating. I always carried notices with the names of towns written on them, and I used lipstick to change the names.'

Bill has an amusing philosophy about hitchhiking which he says is a realistic approach to adopt. 'The man who picks you up is not so much doing you a favour as himself. He is most likely bored with his own company and is trying to stave off sleep or drowsiness. All you do is start talking. When I was in Western Australia I began talking immediately and told drivers my life story. I always asked about their jobs and their families. People love the chance to talk to somebody. They tell you things which don't have to mean very much but nobody cares because you may never meet these people again.

'All my life I have had a spirit of adventure and that is not going to die until they put me into a coffin.'

Bill runs me the few miles out to the Durrus turnoff which gives me an encouraging start to the Mizen peninsula. On the way he tells me of a saying which he heard on his travels in Afghanistan more than thirty years ago: *All the world loves two types of people: a lover and an adventurer.*

Bill bids me farewell at a T-junction at Tedagh three miles along the main Bantry to Ballydehob road. I throw my ruck against the ditch and inside five minutes am on my way again.

The Mizen peninsula has remained largely unpeopled and undesecrated. Mass at the Sacred Heart Church in Durrus, where I'm dropped, has ended and the village is busy cooking its Sunday lunch. O'Brien's foodstore is the nerve centre of the place, but with the exception of Casey's, the five other bars are empty. It is one of those rare days when the sun is throwing off a glorious heat haze which settles over the shops, bars and houses. Nobody seems to want to bathe in the sunshine and everywhere there is that Sunday afternoon feeling of emptiness and lethargy. I feel like rousing the village from its sunny slumbers. I want to climb on to the steps of the pink painted Carrigboy National School and like Robin Williams in the film *Dead Poets Society* 'shout my barbaric yawp across the rooftops of the world.' But it occurs to me that there is no point in exhausting my lung power. Nobody would pay a blind bit of attention. The village would continue with its lunch, and anticipation of the big event of the sporting calendar, the football semi-final on television.

Compared with the Kerry peninsulas the Mizen in County Cork is a relatively small one. I consider trying to get to Crookhaven which is at the southern end and spending the night there but rule it out as being too difficult to hitch from the next morning. The man who took me to Durrus said the tip of the peninsula, comprising the villages of Barley Cove and Crookhaven, is sometimes referred to as 'God's pocket.' When my lift comes, with an English couple touring west Cork, I opt to sit with them round the main circular ring of the peninsula through Toormore and up to Schull.

They say they're enjoying their holiday and have been told that the main language in west Cork now is not English, nor even Irish, but in fact German.

'The Germans seem to be everywhere,' the driver hisses. 'They own and run several hotels and restaurants and have holiday homes all over the place. You can't avoid them wherever you go in this area.'

True enough. Two energetic German youths run Andy's restaurant in

Schull. Andy, the owner, tells me they came to live here three years ago although their mother had already been living in the area for more than ten years. They love the purity of the air and cleanliness of the sea for diving. On a good day he says it is comparable to the crystal clear blueness of the Caribbean. With just a slight hint of irony Andy says west Cork is now becoming crowded with foreigners or blow-ins. Employment is not easy to find and it is a question of everyone for him or herself. He says the area attracts many arty and eccentric people as well as intellectuals from both Britain and Europe and it is not hard to see why. Many of them come on a visit and fall in love with the place.

'They call it the Irish Riviera and there are what you might call some upmarket hippies living in this area,' he says. 'They tend to spend most of their time smoking in caravans somewhere along the sea front, moving on when they get tired of the views and dabbling in painting or writing.

'Everyone likes it for the high quality of life, the absence of crime and the sociability of the people. It is far from parochial, and the locals accept us as visitors. After a while here you are no longer a stranger, but become part of the scene.'

Schull is said to mean '*a place of scolbs*' which are sticks used for thatching, although another possible meaning is '*school.*' When I arrive in the late afternoon the village has a subdued atmosphere, but there is more life about it than Durrus.

At the harbour the sailing club has presented the local community with an anchor which was salvaged off Mizen Head in the nineteenth century. It is believed to have come from one of the French fleet which sheltered in the area in the period between 1796-1798. Oystercatchers and curlews provide a hullabaloo. Through my binoculars I spot two shags with their greenish sheen feeding out in deeper waters. In the harbour *The Electric Wave, Golden Eye, Doreen E* and *Susie Wong* all rest peaceably. Out to sea lies a group of one hundred islands, known as the Carbery Hundred Isles. A few are inhabited but most are visited only by birds, or bird watchers.

I check in for the night at Station House, a rambling detached B & B on the edge of the village at the foothills of Mount Gabriel. I walk back into the centre and in the Marine Bar in High Street try to find some information about a boat around Cork. But no-one knows or cares much about the city. A man asks if I've ever heard of the 'People's Republic of west Cork,' and then he tells me I'm in it. Cork city is only eighty miles east, but it might as well be eight thousand.

PROSPER LEAVES HIS MARK

Schull to Youghal

A deep Monday morning depression is settling over Cork and it has nothing to do with the weather. It has more to do with the fact that Kerry beat Cork in the Munster football semi-final by two points. Kerry 1.10 – Cork 0.11 was the final score. The worst imaginable result has happened. It is a black Monday for Corkonians.

KERRY BACK IN THE ASCENDANCY AS CORK REIGN ENDS screams the headline in the *Cork Examiner*. The paper says Kerry gunned down the critics as they were the underdogs and had been vastly under-rated. For five years Cork, who were the favourites to win, dominated Munster football and were reigning champions.

The driver of my first lift, bringing me the five miles from Seaview Terrace outside Schull to Ballydehob, wasn't impressed with the Cork performance.

'I'm really ashamed to call myself a Cork man after the way the team played in that match,' he says. 'The players went to Killarney on the Friday night and were living it up in the hotels for two nights instead of acting as disciplined and trained sportsmen. They were actually celebrating the fact they had got to the semi-final. But they looked a bedraggled team who seemed as though they couldn't care if they ever won another match.

'I'm just glad I didn't go to the trouble of driving all the way up to Killarney and battling through crowds to watch that shambles of a game.'

From Ballydehob the little towns of west Cork are spaced out on the map in almost mathematical succession – ten miles apart. The coast of Cork, from Crow Head to Youghal Bay, is festooned with small seaports, bays, headlands, indentations, harbours and peninsulas trailing out to sea.

Some of the towns on my route touch the squiggly line of the shore, others are a mile or two inland. I will be reasonably satisfied if by this evening I get as far as, or at least within striking distance, of Kinsale or the nearby village of Summer Cove which sounds an inviting place.

Approximately one hour later standing at or about the same oak tree on the outskirts of Ballydehob I revise my expectations. As Frank Richards might have put it in the words of one of his famous characters, Huree Jamset Ram Singh, '*the satisfactoriness of Skibbereen might prove terrific.*' The thought of the Billy Bunter books strikes a memory chord and spurs my mind into action. Could I, I wonder, name the five members of the Harry Wharton gang? How many other characters from the books which I'd first read at the age of nine or ten, could I name? Mr. Quelch with his gimlet eyes, Vernon-Smith or Smithy, Lord Mauleverer, Coker and Potter, Fisher T. Fish, Mr. Prout, that ass Skinner . . .

Funny the things that come into your head at the side of the road to keep dementia at bay. All the way down the west coast from Ballyshannon to Ballydehob I've been standing on the edge of these 'bally' towns for hours. The most lively Bally town to be stuck in I figure would be Ballyhooley, which promised much but according to locals doesn't live up to its name. I consult my place names book. Six of its eighty pages are given over to places with the prefix 'bally.' Between Ballyaghan, meaning '*Eochagan's townland*' and Ballywillin, '*townland of the mill*,' are a total of one hundred and sixty. The book says the Irish word '*baile*' means a town, village or townland. Bally is the first element of over five thousand townland names but it does not, on its own, actually name any particular place. I think of a few more: Ballyslapamuckery; Ballygobackwards; Ballyamstuckhere; Ballygetmeoutofhere. At least I'm now rounding the south-west corner and crossing east over the southern section of the country where it could reasonably be hoped the going might be easier and the traffic heavier.

By half-eleven I'm at last on my way from Ballydehob, '*the entrance of the two mouths*' to Skibbereen. Alex Hogan, a restaurateur who also owns a charter boat company in the area, is a gregarious man. He is keen to sell me the idea of an activity holiday in west Cork and pushes a wad of leaflets and information sheets into my hand. They deal with the business he operates and give details of the yacht available for hire and the house overlooking Schull where clients stay. He runs a thirty-six foot ketch, *Sandy Ways*, which he hires complete with a skipper and food. Customers spend a week putting in to harbours along the coastline and are given instruction on navigation.

'I've only started it this year and it is building up slowly,' he says. 'I aim to offer the best facilities available and the ketch is equipped with a satellite

navigation system, VHF radio, a cellnet telephone and full safety specifica-
tion. We also use the services of a trained cordon bleu cook from the
Ballymaloe Cookery School. You can stay on the yacht or in a bungalow
where there is a sauna room, fax machine, satellite TV, a video recorder and
a hi-fi system. The cruising idea appeals to all types of people.'

End of free advertisement. It isn't all that good a lift.

Alex describes west Cork as a haven for artists and people wishing to
develop skills. 'You have to use your initiative to survive as the whole of
west Cork is without any major industry. Unemployment and emigration
are at high levels. We have an enormous number of craft and design shops
here. People run their own studios, workshops and galleries, and the big
thing is to make your own pottery, stoneware or porcelain.'

Alex drops me in the market town of Skibbereen. A large sign at the
one end of main street says the town (population 2,130) owes its foundation to the sack of Baltimore. The residents of that besieged place moved
inland for safety. The original settlements were known as Bridgetown and
Stapleton which grew into the present town of Skibbereen. The famine of
the 1840s severely affected the district. The sign says the local paper, *The
Skibbereen Eagle*, came to prominence in the nineteenth century when it
declared it was keeping its eye on the tsar of Russia.

In the tourist information office I am met with blank stares by two girls
when I enquire about a boat to circumvent Cork city. A more senior
information woman, with a green and white uniform, gives me a quizzical
look. She declares that it is not possible to get a boat of any description
across Cork harbour as there is no service. Furthermore, she expounds, I
am wasting my time – and presumably her time – by asking. I politely
point out I already know there is no service and didn't need to come here
to be told that. A further enquiry about accommodation at Summer Cove
draws another blank. The woman has never heard of Summer Cove until
I point it out to her on my map.

Disgruntled at the lack of any information and assistance I press on
towards Clonakilty as I've a long way still to go to get to Summer Cove.
I'm picked up by a teacher called Des, who says that, like some of his
pupils, he is happy to scheme a few classes for the afternoon. Unlike the
Bord Fáilte workers he is a mine of information on the area, particularly the
historical aspects of it. He points out some landmarks along the way and
tells me about three bronze age standing stones at a place called Gurranes
near Castletownshend.

'They can be found easily by crossing the fields in the opposite direction
to the signpost for Knockdrum fort and the site is certainly well worth
visiting some time,' Des says. 'In fact there used to be five stones there, but
there are now only three and they are known as the Three Fingers.'

Des is going to Clonakilty. On our way through Leap, which he says is pronounced Lep, he tells me there is a saying, 'Beyond the Leap, Beyond the Law.' The name refers to a leap performed by a legendary character called Donavon across a narrow gorge which is now hidden by the main road. Near Clonakilty we pass a road with a sign pointing to the Four Alls. Des says it is a public house a few miles down the road near where Michael Collins, the General of the Free State Army, was born in 1890.

'It is a very old pub and has been there for maybe two hundred years. The name came about because of four pictures which hang inside. There is one of a soldier who says "I fight for all", a priest saying "I pray for all", a king saying "I rule all" and a farmer saying "Ah – I pay for all." So they have come to be collectively known as the Four Alls.'

Clonakilty, Des informs me, is trying not to be outdone by other towns and is building its own local history centre. It will concentrate on the recent past, particularly the period from 1935 to 1945. The idea is to make a scale model of the main landmarks of the region during that period. He says the first scheme involves building a life-size replica of the railway station as it looked during the Second World War.

The main street of Clonakilty seems to stretch on for ever. It is in fact five streets which merge into each other. Oliver Plunkett Street and Pearse Street run into Ashe Street which in turn leads to Wolfe Tone Street and Strand Road. The whole thoroughfare, from the Hair Studio at the western end, to the Animal Health Centre on the other side of town, is nearly two miles. And I have to walk another mile out of town to the Timoleague turnoff from the main road.

Waiting for a lift, I write a few postcards. According to the calculations in my notebook I have now passed the one thousand mile mark and reckon this is cause for celebration. The message is the same on all my postcards: '1,020 miles gone – only 480 to go.' If I make it to Kinsale or Summer Cove by evening I will have a small celebration involving some decent food and a glass or two of wine. After all it's not every day you celebrate hitchhiking a thousand miles.

All along this route I have been trying to find more information about boats to Cobh from the west side of Cork harbour. I have several contact telephone numbers, and make a couple of calls to John Barry who I was told may operate a boat from Passage West to Cobh. Someone else had given me the name Jim White who runs a boat from Monkstown. In both cases I have no luck.

My next lift is with another teacher, Pearse, who takes me through Ballinspittle, the home of the moving statue. The statue was 'discovered' in July 1985. Pearse says it was first seen by a couple of local publicans who were *Fine Gael* supporters, but when there was a change of government the statue stopped moving. Nowadays it doesn't get the vast numbers of people who visited it in the early days. The novelty it appears has worn off.

Summer Cove lies on the other side of Kinsale harbour. It consists of the Bulman Bar, the Boathouse restaurant and half a dozen whitewashed cottages, some with extensions. A tourist board plaque commemorates its moment of historic greatness:

> *It was here during the siege of Kinsale in 1601 and after Ringcurran Castle had been captured, that the English ships landed guns and supplies for the besieged army. Looking across the harbour you may see St. James' Fort and the Blockhouse.*

Outside the bar a red-setter has found a warm place to sleep. The water laps in to a small area of shingle, and on the other side of the harbour, Kinsale – the oldest town in Ireland – sits proud and colourful. Its houses, bathed in gentle evening sunlight, glow pink, orange, red, rust and yellow. Shafts of light shoot down through the evening clouds as two trawlers drift off to fishing grounds.

The problem with Summer Cove is that, apart from a youth hostel, there are no hotels or guest houses. Its identity is smothered by living in the shadow of Kinsale but it doesn't seem to mind that. Half a mile back towards Kinsale I discover an area called Scilly. It is a scattering of a few houses perched above the harbour and I find a room in a guest house here for the night. It is a double room but the woman of the house charges me only the price of a single.

Kinsale has won a host of awards for its appearance. It was the 'tidy towns' winner in 1986 and was nominated by the tourist board for the *Entente Florale*, a competition involving seven European countries. The entrants are judged on the use of trees, flowers and shrubs to improve the environment.

More than any other town I've come through, Kinsale has gone to extreme lengths to make itself look smart. Flower boxes and hanging baskets everywhere enhance the appearance of the place. Every conceivable type of container is utilised to hold flowers. Beer kegs, barrels, kettles, concrete bollards, pots, skillets, flat bottomed bastibles, and even sections of boats are bursting with lobelia, marigolds, pansies, petunias, begonias and a range of other bedding plants. Every nook, every cranny, every hole, and every window ledge is seen as a place for hanging, trailing or displaying flowers. As I stroll around the town I reflect that places like Portrush and Bundoran could do well to take a leaf, or shrub, from the Kinsale book to try to improve their image.

As well as its floral extravaganza Kinsale, which is twinned with Antibes, is also known as the gourmet capital of Ireland. A group of twelve restaurants have come together to form a good food circle. During a gastro-ramble to check on some of the menus on display I look in through windows at crowds of happy looking people tucking into their food. Mouth-watering aromas emanate from the premises. The culinary range available would make even Egon Ronay happy. You can have breast of woodpigeon marinated in red wine; stir fried rabbit with noodles; pink calf's liver; confit of duck with pineapple and cassis sauce; crab en choux which is choux pastry puffs filled with white crabmeat and served with crab toes in a creamy tarragon sauce; Kinsale smoked fish or wings of fire – chicken wings in a hot pirri pirri sauce. I'm glad I've already made up my mind to splash out here.

Before eating it is imperative to sort out the arrangements for a boat to Cobh. The next hour is spent ringing directory enquiries, going through the phone book, chasing leads and following up the names of people I'd been given along the road. I'd gathered a variety of information dealing with boats but hadn't made any progress. I finally discover the name of John Foley, personnel officer of Irish Steel whose plant is on Haulbowline Island at Ringaskiddy. After a couple of telephone calls I track him down at his home and he suggests I present myself at the premises at twelve-thirty tomorrow afternoon when he says I will be able to take one of the ferries used to carry the workers to and from Cobh.

In part celebration of this, and the fact that I have now topped the one thousand mile mark, I spend the rest of the evening modestly living it up in Hoby's restaurant. My scintillating meal comprises hot buttered oysters, followed by baked wild salmon and a couple of glasses of the house white. It's a night of excellent food. The restaurant has a cheerful ambience and is a firm believer of the 'music while you eat principle.' The repertoire is made up of old established favourites. I don't know if it has anything to do with the fact that there are no men working in the restaurant but they seem to favour the sound of the female voice here. Ella Fitzgerald sings *Ev'ry Time We Say Goodbye* and *I Get a Kick Out of You*. The first lady of song is followed by Vera Lynn with *Lily Marlene* and *A Nightingale Sang in Berkeley Square*, and the evening is rounded off with the unique vocal style of Aretha Franklin singing *You're all I need to Get By*.

The highlight of the evening for me though is the pudding of decadent chocolate cake; taken as a whole the meal certainly makes up for eighteen days of generally indifferent food.

* * * * *

On the face of it my schedule for the morning looks a simple one. I need to cover the twenty miles to Haulbowline Island by twelve-thirty. It is a cross country route involving lifts to Fivemilebridge, Carrigaline and over to Ringaskiddy. The first half of the trip is in a van with Padraig Fallon. He runs a grass cutting business and tells me he is one of the few local people to have made some money out of Kinsale and the property boom which has accompanied its prosperity.

Padraig had what he calls a two-up two-down terraced house in Scilly. He bought it for twenty thousand pounds and sold it for sixty-eight thousand. 'It went to an American woman whom I never even met as it was all transacted through letters and on the telephone.'

He now lives in a bungalow on the other side of Kinsale. Padraig is not into flower consciousness. He doesn't have much time for the co-ordinating committees and groups set up to improve the appearance of Kinsale, and believes local people have been put down by outsiders. He can remember when Kinsale was in his words 'nothing but a dump.' He adds though that things have improved. 'Fifteen years ago when the tide came in there was a terrible smell of the raw sewage but they seem to have sorted out that problem. I suppose it is a good town if you like looking at bright flowers all day.'

At Fivemilebridge a small group of ox-eye daisies is growing beside me at the road. The village was so named because it is five miles from the Cork city boundary and five miles from the Owenbue River. It consists of a petrol station, pub and three houses. A short lift takes me another few miles through Carrigaline and I have fifty minutes to hitch the three and a half miles to Ringaskiddy. Within ten minutes a car pulls over and I'm on my way with a man who runs me out the causeway to Haulbowline Island saving me a long walk.

I slip past the security hut at Irish Steel and through an area with signs warning about wearing protective headgear. I walk purposefully looking as though I know where I'm going. The face on the clock tower of the nearby Irish Naval dockyard is twelve-fifteen: perfect timing. Haulbowline is an industrial island made up of warehouses with large sheds of corrugated iron and steel. Smoke pours out of chimneys, and lorries move around shifting steel pipes. Across the water I glimpse Cobh. It has rows of neatly positioned terraces leading back in tiers uphill to St. Colman's Cathedral where the three hundred foot spire dominates everything.

No-one in the steelyard seems in the least concerned about my presence. In the office where the workers clock-in after coming off the ferry from Cobh a poster by the safe attitude poster programme states: *Don't forget to wear your protective gear.* Underneath someone has scrawled in capital letters with a red pen the words: *CONDOMS AVAILABLE IN THE CANTEEN.*

Three naval vessels, docked in the yard, are being checked over by engineers. A fishery protection vessel is preparing to head off on duty into the Atlantic and young men in uniform run around looking busy.

Shortly after half past twelve the *Steel Isle*, an eighty foot vessel arrives to discharge about twenty workers coming on shift. On the return trip to Cobh the only other passenger with me is the sales manager of Irish Steel, Gareth Skidmore. He says they produce molten steel from scrap which is converted into a continuous solid bar and then shaped into the required finished product on a rolling mill. After being cut and bundled it is taken to the dispatch wharf for the overseas market. The firm's main business is in south-west Europe, mostly in the Benelux countries, and Germany and France. There is a small Irish market but it doesn't amount to much.

The journey across Cork harbour into Cobh lasts just four minutes and forty-eight seconds. It had taken more than twelve phone calls to set up but it was worth the effort as the town looks its best seen from the water. A *garda* keeps a close eye on me and my rucksack as I disembark. There is a security watch on all vessels in the area because some of the most danger-ous Irish criminals are behind bars on Spike Island, a green swarded island further out in the harbour.

The *Steel Isle* drops me at pierhead, or what used to be called the White Star Pier, where the transatlantic liners from that famous company left for the United States. The other quays were Cunard Quay, Holland-Ameri-can Quay and Ballast Quay, the latter named from the time when ships without cargo took on stone ballast. The competition from airlines in the 1950s brought the days of travel by liners to a close.

Cobh calls itself the home of sailing as the world's first yacht club, the Royal Cork, was launched into the waters here in 1720. In those days it was known as the 'Water Club of the Harbour of Corke.' The town was renamed Queenstown to mark the visit of Queen Victoria in 1849 and reverted back to Cobh in 1922. There is a long tradition of naval opera-tions here as the large harbour is recognized as being a safe anchorage. During the French and American wars of the eighteenth century British fleets assembled in Cobh, and in the First World War it was the principal base of the American naval forces in Europe.

Over the years Cobh has been a landing place for immigrants and for sailors from visiting ships who later settled in the town. But it was also the point of final farewell for many people leaving in search of a better life elsewhere. For many emigrants it was the last piece of Irish soil they stood on as they waited for their passage to the new world. Today the offices used by Cunard are occupied by *Oifig an Phoist*. Outside the building a bronze sculpture stands as a memorial to *The Lusitania*, the ship which was sunk off Kinsale by a German submarine during the First World War. An angelic looking figure with two men symbolizes the sadness of fishermen when people are drowned at sea.

Cobh is making sure it isn't left out of the heritage/culture/ historic nostalgia boom sweeping the country. The old yacht club building in the harbour is being restored as a cultural centre for the visual arts. It will be renovated to look much as it did in its heyday. Two million pounds is also being spent on turning the town into a theme centre focussing on the wave of emigration from the port and looking at its historical effects.

Behind all this is the grey granite grandness of St. Colman's Cathedral with its limestone buttresses calling out to be visited. It stands aloof and above the small houses, but they also help to soften its image. Rows of terraces with colourful doors surround it. One street, on a steep sloping hill, is known as the 'Deck of Cards.' In my mind's eye I know I've seen this image somewhere before. In San Francisco the city skyscrapers sit behind a row of Victorian terraces in Alamo Square – similar in many ways to this scene. The harbour and bay here has in fact been compared to San Francisco bay – and to stretch a point you could even say Spike Island is the Alcatraz of Ireland.

The dry factual details of the cathedral are as follows: it was built in the French Gothic style; started in 1868 it took forty-seven years to complete; the exterior is of Dalkey granite with dressings of Mallow limestone; the cost was £235,000, of which £90,000 was raised by the people of Cobh; the carillon, with forty-seven bells, is the largest in Ireland; the organ has a total of 2,468 pipes and the cathedral is named after St. Colman (522-604 AD) who is the patron of the Diocese of Cloyne.

Inside, two women pause for silent reflection around the tabernacle and take in the architectural grandeur of their surroundings. The mellow lighting reveals marble pillars, stone arches and delicate carvings. Over one of the confessionals are two faces; they are reputed to be caricatures of the clerk of works, Charles Doran, and were carved by a stonecutter who had been annoyed by his insistence on the highest standards of craftsman-ship. Both faces wear a look of exasperation and annoyance.

From this quiet haven I walk back to the water front. My objective is to make my way from Great Island and join the main Cork-Waterford road, reaching Midleton or Youghal by evening. Beside the railway line leading out of the town, long pointed leaves of red valerian grows in vast quantities. It flourishes at the coast and on cliffs although this is the first time I've seen it. Masses of the rich crimson blossom are all around the town.

Behind me a naval vessel pulls slowly out from Haulbowline Island. The twelve man crew – eight at the prow including the captain and four astern – stand at ease as they pass Cobh on their way to sea. A clerk, working in the administrative offices in connection with naval duties, picks me up. He says this is the traditional protocol for ships leaving port. The vessel is on its way to Germany for a courtesy visit. He seems reluctant to give me any more information on naval operations, and delicately side-steps my enquiries. He fires several questions at me, nodding at my answers but never taking his eyes off the road and making no comment.

He drops me beside a roundabout at the Midleton bypass. This is a busy road taking the traffic to and from the Rosslare ferry and is the main business route to Waterford. But, as I've discovered, these sort of roads are frequently much more difficult for the hitcher. Eventually I'm picked up by a van driver called Eddie on his way to Youghal. His travelling companion is a shaggy dog. As I jump into the front seat on to several cushions the long-haired mongrel slithers over the top of the seat and into the back of the van. His name is Prosper. He sits up with his paws resting on the back of the seat. His tongue is taking an interest in the back of my head about which I feel slightly uncomfortable. I don't like to make an issue of it. Eddie looks at him with affectionate eyes and slaps his head. 'He's something of a hybrid really. He is part collie and part golden retriever. We call him a Heinz dog because he is fifty-seven varieties.' Prosper cocks his head and knows we're talking about him. Eddie says he is a friendly, harmless dog but badly needs a hair cut.

John Steinbeck in *Travels With Charley* notes that a dog, particularly an exotic one, is a bond between strangers. He says many conversations en route begin with 'What degree of a dog is that?' Such is the case in this situation, even though it is a brief friendship over a twenty mile lift.

I've only partly climbed out of the van at the harbour front in Youghal when the hirsute hound bounces back to his cushions. I discover my trousers, T-shirt and rucksack are covered in white hairs. The landlady in the Ferry View B & B provides me with a clothes brush to rid myself of Prosper's unwanted moulting.

Youghal is a place with a past. A tourist board leaflet calls it an historic walled seaport. It is one of those towns, the woman says that gets tourists, but not an over-abundance of them. I note with great pleasure that throughout the length of its narrow main street the chain stores have not infiltrated and it has retained its original shop fronts. There are a few window boxes but it has not been seized by the same floral suffocation as Kinsale. The centre of the town is dominated by the clock tower. It was built in 1776 and was used as a gaol. According to a town trail booklet when the clock tower was built many citizens said it was in every way an 'objectionable intrusion.'

Near the harbour, hidden under trees, is a small commemorative plaque to a schooner which was lost in 1936:

In memory of the crew of the Nellie Fleming, Youghal's last sailing vessel lost with all hands in February 1936 and in memory of all seafarers and fishermen who lost their lives at sea.

Youghal's street names resound with history. Like any self-respecting Irish town conscious of its patriotic past, it has its Parnell Square, Emmet Place, De Valera and Grattan Streets, and to crown it all there's a Cromwell's Arch. But here you will also find little streets and alleyways leading down to the water front with names such as Meat Shambles Lane, Windmill Lane, Fork Lane, Tallow Street, Chapel Lane, Water Lane, Fish Lane and even a Mouse Street.

Top marks must be awarded to the Old Well restaurant where the food is accompanied by a selection of romantic music. *Blue Moon* and *Touch Me In The Morning* bring to a dreamy end another long day on the road and mark the close of my hitchhiking door on Ireland's largest county.

THE END OF AN EMPIRE

Youghal to Dunmore East

The coastal stretch of County Waterford from Youghal Bay to Waterford harbour is punctuated by small holiday resorts and sandy beaches washed with the warm Gulf Stream. Leaving Youghal and County Cork behind me is proving hard. It is one of those roads on which you don't get dawdlers. Businessmen, driving on their own, rush past at speed. They don't have time to acknowledge the presence of hitchhikers, never mind stop for them.

To pass the time I set about cleaning my hair-stained rucksack. Dozens of Prosper's hairs from yesterday still cling to it and it's a laborious job removing them. My hairy rucksack may have something to do with the lack of lifts. I count the number of red beetles crawling over the top slab of a low wall at O'Reilly Terrace on the Dungarvan Road. At least twenty are making their way over and around small pieces of moss and stones. The tiny beetles are just about identifiable, while the bigger ones with their two large tentacles at the front and four at the side, move faster and with more agility. They seem to go only in an anticlockwise direction and don't apparently believe in travelling in a straight line. Maybe they're trying to tell me something. In Irish mythology beetles are said to be lucky. I could use some luck right now.

The wildlife pleasures are further rewarded with the arrival overhead of a yellowhammer. The slim bird with its yellow head and breast crouches on top of a television aerial singing loudly from its perch.

A man gives me a lift as far as a bridge over the Blackwater River, a few miles out of Youghal and across the county boundary into Waterford. I consult my watch and map. It is almost eleven-thirty and I have travelled only three miles. I now appreciate what somebody once told me about hitchhiker's having to take the rough with the smooth. It is a strange activity in its own way. One moment you have solitude and loneliness and the next you are in someone else's car. I've heard about various tricks hitchhikers use to try to get cars to stop. These include ploys such as a girl kneeling down to pray in the middle of the road; another who wore a T-shirt which said 'So Many Men, So Little Time,' and the ingenious plan of a man who always carried an empty petrol canister.

I stick to the tried and tested method of using my thumb, undoubted good looks, and personal charisma. Dozens, scores and what probably amounts to hundreds of cars continue to drive past at speed. Today's travels, I had hoped, would take me along the coast of Waterford through Tramore into Dunmore East and beyond into County Wexford. The way things are looking I might have to settle for Dungarvan. Like so many other days I can't make any plans for later in the evening.

If it was up to me to award rosettes for gushing prose and superlatives in tourist board booklets, then the moving finger which wrote the Dungarvan entry would feature amongst the very highest, if not the first:

> *The magnificent approaches to Dungarvan on all sides inject the traveller with expectation and that expectation is fulfilled for Dungarvan town and port shields not just the physical remains of a great past but a current linguistic survival which of itself, in the wake of such intensive westernisation, must be estimated a miracle of sorts.*

The moving finger writes with wondrous word power but for me it's the wonder of the moving thumb which finally attracts a van. With all the speed I can muster I sprint to the van and climb into the front seat. I have worked hard and waited long for this lift. If the driver had told me he was going only five hundred yards I would have broken his leg to travel even that distance with him. As it is he takes me through superb rolling countryside. The Monavullagh Mountains rise in the background and behind, running through central Waterford, stretch the Comeraghs. The driver, from Oxfordshire, is on a trip to Ireland mixing work with pleasure. He has been delivering furniture in Cork and is on his way back to his wife in their holiday home at the foot of the Comeragh Mountains.

After lunch in Ormond's cafe in Dungarvan I make my way across the bridge over the River Colligan past the Moresby Buoy and on to the coastal road to Tramore. The buoy was erected in 1988 to the memory of *The Moresby* which foundered in Dungarvan Bay on Christmas Eve, 1895 with the loss of twenty lives.

Past rows of detached houses with neat privet hedges I settle down to what I reckon will be another long haul to Tramore. It is described in my guide as having more than fifty acres of amusement parks which, not having any children in tow, seems a good reason for pushing on through it. However, to get to Dunmore East, Tramore is unavoidable. A man cycles past and shouts that I'm wasting my time waiting for a lift on this road. I stick it out. An hour passes. It feels like a lifetime. It is turning out to be a hopeless day for lifts. One of the worst yet. But suddenly, and without warning – for such is the peril facing the hitchhiker – a Nissan Patrol speeds around the corner and stops.

John Vanderpol, from East Holland, is on his way to Waterford city via Tramore. He has the best job of anyone I have met so far. He is a landscape design architect who spends six months of the year in Ireland and six months in the Netherlands. During the winter at home he draws up plans and landscapes country parks and play areas. In May each year John comes with his wife and family to his holiday home on the south coast of Ireland where he spends the summer, returning to Holland again at the end of October. He bought his holiday cottage at Ardmore for twenty thousand pounds several years ago and enthuses about Ireland.

'I like the quality of life in this area and the water in Ireland is excellent. My children have already been in the sea swimming several times this year. There are, of course, certain things I love about Holland, but I am happy to be there during the winter when it is colder and when I am working in an office for most of the time.'

John drops me at Summer Hill in Tramore. It has all the appearance of a town dressed up for the benefit of tourists and visitors. Appropriately the name means '*great strand*' and there is at least three miles of it spread around the bay. About fifty people are spaced along its length. Most are huddled against the wall at the back of the beach and a few young girls jump the waves taking advantage of the dry day.

Elsewhere most interest centres on the fortune of the Irish horse Kooyonga in the three forty-five Coronation Stakes at Royal Ascot. A man in the bookies hands over three hundred pounds, staking his earnings on the Irish jockey Warren O'Conner. No doubt there were some parties later that night when the horse won at three to one.

Tramore in some respects is a mirror image of Portrush at the other end of Ireland. Both resorts have the swell and smell of the Atlantic, and they share a commonality of huge amusement parks, trinket emporia shops and an assortment of dingy-looking pubs and hotels. Tramore is also littered with caravans, holiday homes and bungalows.

The afternoon is turning into a scorcher. After an aimless wander around I resolve to make tracks further along the coast to Dunmore East. The route to Dunmore out of Tramore is my ideal kind of road: a few cars, a hushed atmosphere, no hitchers, slowly melting tarmac, high hedges and swallows dive bombing from trees which look eminently climbable. It's a windless day and the first, apart from day one on the Antrim coast, when I've been able to wear a T-shirt and still feel warm. I wish I'd gone into the shop in Tramore where you can have your own message written on one. Mine would have read 'Too Many Bloody Businessmen, Too Little Time.'

* * * * *

Dunmore East is in a huff with the tourist board. It all stems from the fact that a map, with more than two hundred towns and villages, was produced by the board and sent to anglers throughout Britain and Ireland. Dunmore East was left off the map and local people were not amused. It was a glaring omission. Along with the neighbouring village of Passage East the residents felt overlooked.

Dunmore is a village in two parts. The lower area has an hotel and cafe with a few thatched cottages near the beach. Up the hill in the direction of the harbour, white-pink houses and a selection of hotels, restaurants, shops and guest houses are spaced along the road. The harbour was built in 1814 to cater for the growth of the village as a centre for the herring industry. It used to be the mail packet station for Waterford and during the nineteenth century developed as a fashionable resort for the wealthy merchants of the city.

I arrive just in time to catch the start of an important beachside ceremony: the raising of the blue flag award for the cleanliness and quality of the beach. About forty local bigwigs, including the Mayor of Waterford, representatives of the business community, tourism groups, local residents, the clergy and the media are there for the presentations. Silver starfish awards are handed over for the consistently high quality of the bathing water in the area. A press release from the Irish coastal environment group says the sampling throughout the season showed that the water quality never once breached EC guidelines. Only thirty-nine beaches in Ireland have received this award.

After the ceremony I am invited to the Strand Hotel where a celebration is getting into full swing. Food and drink is served in copious amounts. Noel McDonagh, of the Residents' Association, tells me about the row over the village being left off the map. He says there was a great deal of annoyance when the map was produced and Dunmore was not included.

'Many people felt the tourist board were not doing enough to promote the south-east and were concentrating too much on the western seaboard of Ireland,' he says. 'That map was distributed to anglers all over this country and in Britain. It was a disgrace that we were left off and we told the board that in no uncertain terms. They said they would rectify the situation as soon as they could.'

Noel explains that Dunmore is at a crossroads in its development. It appeals to people who don't want to go to Tramore, and it has always regarded itself as a more sophisticated resort. 'We don't want to see any amusement parks or arcades built here. If people want that they only have to drive eight miles over to Tramore to get their fill of it.'

Noel says they are trying to attract more fishermen to the area. Dunmore is a fishing village and the catches include delicacies such as lobster and crayfish. 'The fishing industry has grown very big in the past ten years and we now have one of the largest fishing fleets in Western Europe with more than fifty boats,' he says. 'However the past season was poor for fishermen. There was a drop of thirty per cent in the catches. The trouble with this place is that people have a tendency not to tackle problems, but to rest on their laurels.'

Noel wants to see more naval vessels operating in the area. There are just eight vessels and they carry out pollution control, security duties and emergency services in connection with the lifeboat. He says the EC should provide more. 'We patrol forty per cent of the waters with Irish boats and they should be doing more to help us.'

On the future for Dunmore, Noel insists there is too much haphazard development. 'We want, as far as possible, to keep the old image of the village, but holiday homes are increasing in the area and building is gathering pace all the time. It is crucial that we don't upset the zoning balance of housing throughout this area. Development has been far too rapid for the good of the place.'

Dunmore is clearly one of those villages which has thought carefully about its development. Sited behind trees at either end of the village the two caravan parks are hidden from view. They represent examples of thoughtful planning. The visitor could easily pass by without noticing them.

In the main bar of the hotel the party is gaining momentum. Noel introduces me to some of Dunmore East society. And it's at this point that the KGB pounce on me. It is said that to slip into the hands of the KGB can be one of the most terrible fates to befall anyone visiting the village. Apparently they keep a low profile most of the year, but when they do emerge from the undergrowth anything can happen.

The KGB is a group of three men. Their mission tonight in Dunmore East entails the consumption of a certain amount of Russian vodka. They are more interested in that than in anything to do with espionage, foreign intelligence gathering or secret operations. For them the doctrines of Stalin, Brezhnev or even Gorbachev don't hold much interest.

In reality there is nothing all that sinister about the KGB being here. The inner portals of the Kremlin would not mean much to them. They haven't got the demeanour, and two-thirds of them aren't the required height. Far from being a ruthless group of state security policemen they are a triumvirate of immaculately dressed and gregarious hoteliers. Their surnames automatically give the game away. John Kelly, Brendan Gallagher and Charlie Boland have grouped themselves under the collective banner of the KGB.

They take me under their wing. After a session of close questioning and a covert checkover they say I am free to remain in the Strand where the drink is flowing in ever greater quantities. I'm handed a cocktail in a tall glass and told to drink it. I ask what's in it. One of the KGB men, Charlie, says it contains vodka, tia maria and coke. He smiles and says they have a special name for it. I hazard a guess. 'Is it a Black Russian?'

'Nope,' says Charlie, 'we call it The Fall of the Soviet Empire.' He says the KGB meets every so often, but without any planned agenda. Tonight's celebration of the blue flag and silver starfish awards is the perfect excuse for them to come together. Charlie says there are some similarities with their Soviet counterparts.

'We regard ourselves, like the real KGB, as an élite and select group but we pride ourselves on the fact that, unlike them, we have never had any defections.'

They have though had requests for membership. The owner of the hotel where the party is taking place once tried to get into the KGB. Charlie flashes me another grin. 'His name is Mike Fox and he comes from Connemara, so we had a lot of difficulty explaining to him that he could not join our group as there is no 'F' in KGB. We suggested he should form his own organisation and call it the FBI but it never got off the ground.'

Charlie pushes another 'Fall of the Soviet Empire' into my hands. He raises his glass. 'Here's to Ireland and all who hitchhike round her,' he says.

I smile and clink my glass against his, offering my own toast. 'Here's to the KGB and I hope *The Skibbereen Eagle* is keeping its eye on you all.'

Charlie tells me that on the Waterford side there is a place near Passage East called Crooke. He says the phrase 'by hook or by crook' originated there during the time of Cromwell. He is reputed to have said he would take Waterford city either by landing on Hook Head or on the opposite side of the Suir Estuary at Crooke.

By midnight the men of the KGB are in boisterous mood. The bar shows no sign of closing. There is a rumour of a late licence but no confirmation is established. The bar has filled with gate crashers, hangers on and socialites. My glass has been refilled many times. Several elegantly dressed women just returned from the early summer sales at Brown Thomas in Dublin's Grafton Street sip brandies. The trio of KGB men have found spoons and other utensils and begin an impromptu music session. Their favourite song appears to be *Back in the USSR*. For the next two hours everything from *Me and Bobby McGee* to *When I'm Sixty-Four* is given a rousing airing and standing ovation by the ever-growing crowd.

At half past two the men of the KGB are in disarray. The Soviet Empire has fallen here as well. Last drinks are served and the final choruses sung. I slip unnoticed out a back door. The night air is soft and warm. I creep off in search of my guest house where I tiptoe up the stairs to bed and quickly fall into a deep sound sleep.

INVESTIGATING BASTARDSTOWN

Dunmore East to Courtown

The perfect cure after an evening of conviviality and music spent in the company of the KGB men of Dunmore East is a gentle wind and strong sun beating down on the head and neck. It has a remarkably sobering effect.

Before leaving I saunter about the village in a fairly fragile state, hoping the morning sun and fresh air will waken me. From Dunmore I wish to hitch up to Passage East, take the ferry to Ballyhack and try to get down to Kilmore Quay on the south Wexford coast. The ferry is the quick route into County Wexford and cuts out Waterford city.

A brief lift with a woman, her daughter and their red-setter called Zebedee, takes me the few miles to a crossroads where the road forks to the right for Passage East. I sit on the grass verge glad not to have to converse with anyone for a while. Two birds call quietly in a distant field. A tractor with a load of hay on its trailer passes back and forth a few times and the countryside smells wash across me.

I'd like a lift on the trailer but it is only going a quarter of a mile. 'Uncle Mark' once said that riding aloft on a mountain of fragrant hay is the earliest form of the human pleasure excursion:

For utter joy and perfect contentment it stands alone in a man's threescore years and ten; all that come after it have flaws, but this has none.

I've drifted off into a world of my own but am quickly brought back to the reality of the bitumen and fields of east Waterford with a lift from a retired couple who live near Fermoy in County Cork. They are on a short break and spent the night in Dunmore but escaped the clutches of the KGB.

117

Dennis and Bridie Broderick are heading across on the ferry but aren't sure where they want to go. They'd thought about driving out to Hook Head when they reached the other side but say they have no firm plans. When I mention the possibility of going to Kilmore Quay Dennis agrees to take me as he has never been there.

From Ballyhack – a village full of snug little squares – we pass through a series of hamlets which are as sleepy as I feel. I've lapsed into a sort of catatonic trance and my headache, if anything, worsens. The green fields are sparkling in the sun and the heat smothers me when I step out of the car. The intensity of the light is dazzling.

I have determined this is going to be an afternoon of rest. I check into one of Kilmore Quay's thatched cottages which is run as a B & B. After taking several aspirins I book my place on the hot beach and spend a couple of hours recouping last night's lost sleep.

* * * * *

I'm wakened by a Swedish couple who've set up their telescopes on tripods near me on the beach to view the birds across from here on the Saltee Islands. The islands are known as 'seabird city.' The *siesta* has helped my headache and I join them in their search of the birdlife. The Swedes are especially keen to find the roseate tern, the rarest breeding seabird in Britain and Ireland. They say many bird watching friends of theirs come to Ireland on what they call an 'ornitholiday' to try to find the seabird. The colonies are usually situated on islands. The roseate terns elude our search and the Swedes conclude the only way to find them is to take a boat to the islands, or travel slightly further east, to Lady's Island Lake in the morning.

Kilmore Quay is a village embedded to the sea. The fishermen are absorbed by it and the village depends on it for its survival. It supports four fish factories and the exporting of fish is big business. The first fishermen's co-operative in Ireland was formed here. Practically every family has a connection with the fishing fleet or the lifeboat. The woman in charge of the lightship *Guillemot* which is a maritime museum on display at the pier says the lifeboat at Kilmore Quay is one of the busiest in Ireland. It has saved over a hundred lives since its foundation. Most launches, she says, are to help the commercial and fishing craft so it has a big area of responsibility.

The *Guillemot* has serviced many stations around Ireland over the years as part of the lightship function. In the late sixties she was brought to Wexford and converted into a museum. The maritime society in Kilmore Quay bought her and berthed her at their harbour where she has proved a big attraction. On board is an extensive collection of maritime pictures, ship models and sea antiques.

Kilmore Quay is a remarkably well preserved place. Sixteen thatched houses survive along the main street. The village overlooks the Bay of Ballyteige and then gives way to a fringe of sandhills stretching for miles along the coast. It is twinned with Crehen in north-east Brittany lying just across the Atlantic Ocean.

I have come to Kilmore Quay on a mission. I want to investigate how the nearby townland of Bastardstown got its name. On my Ordnance Survey map it lies two miles east of Kilmore Quay along the coast. Several people in the village tell me the man who can give me information about Bastardstown is Jack Devereaux who lives near the harbour.

I've no trouble finding his house. The door is opened by a tall man with a slight stoop. He looks me over, and when I tell him I'm in search of information on townland names he smiles and brings me into the living room. Jack lives on his own in a spartan but pleasant house. He says he's delighted to have a visitor. He sinks into a deep comfortable chair near the window. He tells me his son, who lives a couple of doors away, is coxswain of the lifeboat and the sea runs deep in the family history. They were Normans and came originally from Everux in Normandy. Jack says there was a big Norman influence in the area and the region had its own local dialect, a kind of Middle English, which has now died out. He cites examples of phrases or words which were still common when he was a boy. 'If you were caught looking out through a window or in through the keyhole of a door you were *keeking*,' he laughs.

He recounts a host of other phrases, rubbing his chin every so often to refresh his memory. 'If you squat down on your haunches you *curk* down. *Zeven* is *dhen* minus *dhree*, a *cowm* is used to shape your hair and the *tyel* is that part of the cow that wags at the back.'

The local dialect covered the two baronies of Bargy and Forth and was known as *Yola*, meaning old as in *Yole Teoun*, old town. Jack sighs heavily. 'It is a pity the dialect died out. One of the last men who could speak it fluently was Pat Murphy. He lived in St. Vaux in Carn and died in 1926.'

On the question of how Bastardstown came to be so named Jack believes the story goes that there was a family in the area called either Baastard or Bas'tard. He thinks it may have been an old Irish name that was mixed up and became the name of a townland.

'There is nothing to be seen there now except a road leading down to the sea.' He says the area has been eroded over the years by the storms and sea. I ask him about some of the other strange sounding names of south Wexford and how they came about. Jack turns his ear round, cups his hand behind it and I repeat the question.

'You think Bastardstown is an odd name, I can see.' He gives me a grin. I nod enthusiastically. 'Well we have a few other funny names here as well.' He puts his hands up. 'But don't ask me how Heavenstown and Horetown got their names because I don't know.'

Jack is eighty-two years old. Apart from a few arthritic and hearing problems he says he can manage well on his own. He certainly looks and sounds alert and there is nothing wrong with his memory or knowledge of toponymics. He has recollections of both good times and bad times in Kilmore Quay.

Jack's voice drops to a whisper as he recalls the events of an evening in December 1989. He stares out the window and is silent for the briefest of moments. 'It was a very odd night. There was no howling wind or anything like that. In fact it was unnaturally calm earlier in the evening. But when the storm blew up at sea the whole coastline was destroyed. What we got that night was the tail-end of a subterranean earthquake. More than a hundred feet of the pier collapsed and was washed away. It fell just like a pack of cards destroying three boats and damaging twenty others. The big stones fell on them and the whole place felt at one stage as if it was going to erupt.

'The village was ravaged. It was left without electricity and water as the mains pipe was ruptured. It was a frightening experience for the people and one which we don't want to go through again in a hurry.'

I thank Jack for his time and information and head off in search of food and the continuation of my quest about Bastardstown. The waitress in the Silver Fox restaurant offers the suggestion that there used to be a large number of unmarried mothers living in the area many years ago and this is how the name originated. She consults the cook and on her return with my cod she relays his rejoinder that the people who live in the area are nothing but a 'shower of bastards over there.'

After dinner I call into the Wooden House Bar, the interior of which is a mini museum to the seafaring life. It used to be an hotel, where in 1916 according to the posters, 'bracing Kilmore was the most fashionable and enjoyable seaside resort in the country.'

The bar, so I read on another poster, can trace its history back to the early 1700s. Over the years it has led a diverse life: shipwrecked sailors were brought in; lobster teas were served; the stout for the bar was bottled on the premises; skippers squared up with crews on Saturday nights; assignations were made and romances flourished.

Notices on the walls give details of how to prevent seasickness by using Lorimer's Cocaine Lozenges in tin boxes for the pocket at one shilling and a penny each. Mr. Lorimer advises all those intending to sail to take his cocaine lozenges. There's also a report of a girl of eighteen who had been

seasick for twenty-four hours and tried cocaine with a '*truly magical effect*.'
I sincerely wished I had had some of the lozenges for the trip to the Aran
Islands last week.

The photographs on the wall are an important part of the decor. They
reflect the robust maritime tradition of the people of Kilmore Quay from
the age of schooners through the days of the yawls and Galway hookers up
to the present trawlers.

A man in the bar has several theories about Bastardstown. He says he
once heard sailors were shipwrecked there from Spain. The local people
would not give them any help or assistance and they became known to the
sailors as 'bastards.' He has also heard a different explanation as to how it
got its name. In some fields in the area a flower known as yellow flag used
to grow. It flourished in marshy or wet areas and one of the varieties of the
plant was known as *Bastardii*. The man tells me another delicious snippet
of information about a group of nuns who own a chalet in the area and use
it as a holiday home. But the Sisters of St. John of God did not like the
address. They wanted to add a degree of respectability to it so they
changed it from Bastardstown to Seaview.

The most plausible explanation on the derivation of the name of
Bastardstown comes from Tomás Hayes, a local schoolteacher. He says it
was mentioned as long ago as the time of the Civil Survey of 1650 when it
was spelt Bastardstowne, and it may even have been recorded before that.
He says at the spot there is a high bay – the Irish for high bay is '*Ba-ard*.'

Tomás directs me to Wexford library where he says I should be able to
find more information in the Griffith Chronicles. To do justice to my
research I walk along the beach which is the short route to Bastardstown.
Jack Devereaux is right. There is nothing except a ramp leading down to
the sea, a couple of derelict houses and a marine supplies shop which is
shut. Despite the claim of big seas it is flat and placid and there is no sign
of high waves.

* * * * *

It was entirely to be expected that the twenty-first of June, the longest day
of the year, would produce one of the longest waits of the journey. Getting
to Kilmore Quay was easy, but hitching out of it is not. It is one of those
villages not on the way to anywhere. It sits on a little point of land on its
own. You go to it because you have to. But Kilmore Quay is the sort of
village where I could happily spend a week or two. Its quiet charm grew on
me during my visit. I found it a lovable place, full of surprises, with warm
friendly people.

I reflect on the summer solstice. For the hitchhiker it is just another day. Midsummer may be at the centre of the astronomical year but as far as I'm concerned, until yesterday, I could have been making my trip in midwinter. I like the article in the morning newspaper which suggests the outstanding characteristic of the Irish climate is its variability. It quotes a climatologist:

> *People should not be astonished if June is not good. We happen to be having a poor June right now, but we've had them before. Last year, for instance.*

I have six days to make it home. Six days to hitch roughly three hundred miles up the east coast. I reckon I am just about on schedule, but much will depend on how quickly I manage to circumvent Dublin. If I keep to my average of fifty miles a day then I should make it.

The chorus of screaming herring gulls is all-pervasive this morning. They poke around the harbour wall for bugs and take up a noisy and aggressive stance on the rooftops of houses behind me. The wind carries in the smell of the sea and at the harbour boxes of fish are off-loaded from the trawlers. From there they will be auctioned to the highest bidder.

Pat Keating has been attending the auction and is now on his way back to Wexford. He has driven the sixteen miles to Kilmore Quay this morning because he was getting only twelve pence a pound for ray in Wexford, while in Kilmore Quay he can get fifty pence a pound. Pat, who runs a boat called the St. Vaux, seems to be an expert on what is known as marine garbology or the study of junk at sea. He says trawlers collect everything in their nets and are unselective. 'They catch shells and all sorts of ships' waste. They also pick up rubbish such as plastic cartons, bottles, cans, timber, glass and discarded fishing gear. In fact they've even been known to catch turtles.' He says the situation deteriorates further north along the east coast. 'At this end the sea is not too polluted and is reasonably clean despite the garbage that comes from it. The water clarity is good compared to further along so we are lucky.'

Pat drives me through Piercetown where we join the main Rosslare to Wexford Road. I've now left behind the Atlantic Ocean and am heading round St. George's Channel before meeting the Irish Sea. I'd thought of trying to make it out to the extreme south-east tip at Carnsore Point but Pat says it would be very difficult to hitch there. He advises me to avoid Rosslare as large numbers of hitchhikers disembark from the ferry.

In the Wexford County Library the two sour faced women librarians look somewhat askance when I make enquiries about Bastardstown. With furrowed brows they repeat the name in conspiratorial tones lest any borrowers get the wrong impression of the place. I'd been told by Tomás Hayes to ask for Jarleth Glynn but he is on his lunchbreak. I tell the women I'll come back in an hour's time, and go off in search of a launderette. They look relieved to see me disappearing.

When I return I'm shown the book called *Griffith's Valuation* which gives the general valuation of rateable property in Ireland. Richard Griffith, the commissioner of valuation, was a civil engineer. He produced boundary descriptions and sketch maps of all the townlands and parishes in the country in 1830. The department then valued the townlands and provided the acreages and valuations required for a fair tax system. In 1853 Griffith listed twenty occupiers of property living in Bastardstown. The entry for each of the occupants reads much the same: house, offices and land. The names are well known in the area: Bolger, Kehoe, Cogley and Pierce.

In the *Civil Survey of 1654-1656 for County Wexford* the townland is spelt Bastardstowne in the parish of Kilmore in the barony of Bargy. The survey is published by the Irish Manuscripts Commission and prepared with introductory notes and appendices by Robert C. Simmington. It provides an old English look at the parish of Killmoore and a description of its *meetes* and *boundes*.

The librarian also produces a six volume set called *Hore's Wexford*. It covers the history of the town and county of Wexford from the earliest times to the rebellion of 1798. The history, published in 1901, was compiled from the state papers, public records and manuscripts of the late Herbert F. Hore of Pole Hore in Wexford and edited by his son Philip Herbert Hore. In one volume, covering the period around 1538, there is a brief mention of 'Bastardestown' in the Kilmore Parish, and again in 1548 when it was spelt 'Bastareston.' There is no indication as to how the name originated.

It has been an absorbing afternoon but again time beats me. The library is closing and I head off to collect my rucksack. My aim is Courtown, about twenty miles along the east coast. I've been warned not to expect much traffic as it is a quieter road than the two busier inland routes.

I walk over the seven spans of Wexford Bridge which crosses the Slaney River and first hitch the two miles out to the turnoff for the coastal road. A fierce wind is blowing in across the wide stretch of harbour. Within twenty minutes I'm on my way in a stinking fish van which picks me up at a petrol station. The driver, in soiled and shabby clothes, says he normally doesn't stop for hitchhikers because of the smell in the van, but I tell him I don't mind as I'm only going a couple of miles. He is going to Gorey. I jump out at the turn for Curracloe and Blackwater and take deep gulps of fresh air.

My information on the coastal road is accurate. The cars on the main road to Gorey outnumber the vehicles using my road by twenty-five to one. When the eighth car has passed me that means I have missed the opportunity of two hundred lifts to Gorey. This underlines the classic example of quiet country road versus busier inland one. Still, it's a pleasant evening and I'm not in any particular hurry. Shortly after six o'clock a friendly farmer and his son bring me the ten miles to Blackwater.

The Friday afternoon rush in this area is summed up for me in the name of a boat I'd seen earlier in the day in Kilmore Quay – *The Misnomah*. I take up a position on a hill leading out of the village beside a caravan site. The road ahead, with its high hedges and cow parsley, is a typical narrow country one.

From here it is the Germans who come to my rescue again in a state-of-the-art Peugeot campervan complete with mountain bicycles strapped on to the back. What I love most about the Germans is the seriousness with which they take their holidays and their Guinness. Meissner Detlef from Braunschweig, his wife and young son, have been holidaying in Ireland for nearly three weeks. I'm amused by his description of his trip. He says they have been 'trespassing' in Limerick and Cork. He later says he has also 'transgressed' in Kilkenny and Wicklow.

Meissner is looking for a camp site in the Courtown area. Like me he favours the back roads, where there aren't so many vehicles. Just as well, because his van takes up most of the road and the few cars we meet are forced to pull in to let us pass.

Courtown is a seaside resort. It consists of two hotels, four pubs, a few guest houses, several carry-outs, amusement arcades and shops selling candyfloss which signs proclaim to be the best in Ireland. Teenagers spend their summer evenings playing the cash roulette, each way accumulator and rainbow gambler machines. Their fathers concentrate on the one armed bandits while the bingo sessions are the exclusive preserve of elderly women who are ferried into the town in a never-ending stream of minibuses.

I discover from Jim Murphy (senior) in one of the pubs along the main street that there really is, surprise surprise, nowhere called Courtown. It is made up of a place called Seamount which stretches through to Riverchapel.

The publican describes Jim as an 'absolute landmine of information' on the area. He is known to everyone in Courtown as the Frenchman. This has something to do with the fact that he went through a period one summer of learning some French phrases and took to wearing a black beret which he thought would impress local people and visitors. Meissner, my German friend, whom I'd arranged to meet in the bar, is bemused by Jim.

Courtown appears to be a confederacy of townlands joined together over the River Ounavarra. According to Jim, as well as Ballintray Upper and Lower, there is also Killtella, Kilbride, Glenalock, Ardamine and

Parknacross which are all part of the greater Courtown area . . . but of course Courtown doesn't actually exist.

'Lord Courtown built the harbour and piers but you must understand there is no village called that,' Jim smiles.

Courtown (that's the village listed on my map) is renowned as the driest place in Ireland. Jim says the area along the coast stretching from Kilmichael Point to Cahore Point has been recorded as being one of the driest parts of the British Isles.

'I don't quite know the reason for that but I believe it has something to do with the curl of the hills,' he says. 'You see we're in a basin here surrounded by mountains. We have the Wicklow, the Blackstairs and Dublin Mountains and we never seem to get the rain clouds that they get elsewhere. If it rains it is usually only for a short spell. This place is often contrasted with Clifden which is supposed to be the wettest place according to the Geographic magazine.' I'm pleased to be able to confirm that for Jim.

There is a difference, Jim acknowledges, between the people of south Wexford and those living in the north of the county. 'The people in the south of the county have a greater pride and have more history than we have in this area. But the thing about here is that the locals are good at mixing with visitors and you are never a stranger. That is why it appeals to so many people who keep coming back year after year for their holidays.'

Jim says the region between Kilmuckridge and Blackwater is known as the 'wreckers' coast.' The people who lived there used to attach lights on to donkeys on the beach so that ships would think they were harbours and would run aground when they tried to tie up. The people then jumped on board and looted the ships.

'It's terrible to think what they did in olden times,' Jim reflects. 'It was all a very long time ago but it continued for many years. As far as I'm aware though it was confined to the area south of Cahore Point and thankfully never spread as far as this region.'

I shake hands with Jim and with Meissner who wishes me a 'gut journey.' On the way back to my B & B the storm clouds are gathering over Courtown. Spits of sullen rain start to fall as I search for the front door key. It was bound to happen. Murphy's Law, I suppose.

HALFHANK HEAD AND THE HOORAY HENRIES

Courtown to Howth

For the twenty-third consecutive day I wake under a strange roof in an unfamiliar bedroom. Two deluges of rain dispel the myth that Courtown is the driest place in Ireland. The rain though is an incentive to remain in my warm bed for another half hour and by the time I reach the coast road out to Ballymoney crossroads the showers have eased.

Today I have to face up to an obstacle further up the east coast. It has a population of a million people, it is called Dublin, and I want to avoid it at all costs. My target is to get near the southern boundary of the city by tonight and then tomorrow plot a boating bypass around the urban sprawl. Saturday morning golfers, in their BMWs and Mercedes, pass by on their way to the Courtown course. They give me a selection of sniggers, jeers and incredulous looks which suggest eccentricity or madness, but no lifts. The coastal road here runs parallel with a busier inland one between Gorey and Arklow. According to my map I'll have to join that road later to get through Arklow.

Over the course of the next eighty minutes the cast, in order of appearance, involves a series of short lifts made up of humdrum conversations as follows:

THE POLITICAL ANALYST: Where are you from? The north, eh? I thought so. What's this fella Paisley really like, eh? He's a good speaker and I'll tell you one thing you know where you are with him. He is blunt, but honest. I personally haven't much time for politicians. There are too many hypocrites. I think people down here have certain prejudices about the north, but then that's to be expected isn't it, eh? Politicians live on the backs of the people. It's the same here.

127

THE WEEKEND BRICKLAYER: It's a God-awful country this. I have to work Saturdays to make a living. Nobody thanks you for sitting at home at weekends when you could be earning money. I've got a wife and four young mouths to feed so I need all the work I can get. I must ask the wife when I go home if she'd let me away for a month.

THE OPTIMIST: We don't get many hitchhikers on these roads. Ah yerra, a few walkers but not many people hitching. Not much traffic you see. You want to avoid Dublin? Well your best bet is to try to get to Dun Laoghaire or Dalkey and ask around. Ah yerra, someone will be going. It should be easy enough if you are prepared to hang around for a while and wait for the right boat. Yerra, too bad you weren't here in May 'cos we'd lovely weather the whole month. I hear the forecast is better for tomorrow and I'm sure it'll be a dry day for your boat trip. Yerra, nice talking to you. Good luck.

THE FATHER: (Complete with wife and three children in back of van. She is silent. They are noisy. He complains). You're going round all of Ireland? My God, that's some walk. Do you not get very tired? You're obviously not married because I couldn't see my missus letting me away for a month to gallivant round the country on my own. He looks at his stony faced wife. She snorts, turns her head and looks out the window.

THE JOKER: (High speed talker). You're going round Ireland because you want to know what makes people tick? Well, I'll tell you what makes them tick. They can't help it, they're just like that. Ha! Ha! Did you hear about the two Kerry engineers who were looking for the north coast of Cork? They spent a year digging in fields and rivers around Mallow and said they hoped to find it in another few months.

I've climbed in and out of five vehicles which have brought me on to the main road into Arklow. My progress, like some of the jokes, is tedious and the weather is playing games again. Every ten minutes a fine drizzle re-emerges. I shelter under large trees which are positioned at accommodating intervals.

For all the difficulties of hitchhiking along it, it is nevertheless one of those pleasant country roads wending its way a mile or so inland from the sea. Names with a cosy ring about them adorn signposts. Along the way I come across the pink cuckoo flower, burnet rose with its five-petalled cream flowers, and bunches of red poppies. A magpie sits on the gate of Mucklow Farm and two brown butterflies flit past me at a country house called Fairy Nook.

I make a phone call to a yacht club in Dun Laoghaire and ask about boats on Sunday. The woman at the other end says there is a large celebration planned for tomorrow when boats from all over the Dublin area will gather at the Liffey as part of a carnival. She thinks it might be extremely difficult getting a lift on one as they'll all be crowded. I, on the other hand, take a more positive view of the situation. It's the first I've heard of this event and it could be the break I need.

* * * * *

The Irish tourist board's Wicklow guide describes the forty-eight point two kilometres of coastline as the *'county's silver lining.'* The stretch between Arklow and Wicklow towns includes the broad beaches of Brittas Bay, Jack's Hole and the Silver Strand where Dubliners spend many of their summer weekends sunning themselves in what they classify as 'their back garden.'

Arklow, which stands at the mouth of the Avoca River, was an important Danish settlement in the ninth and tenth centuries. The town supports a maritime museum but the curators don't believe in opening on Saturday afternoons. The woman in the library next door says the hours are erratic.

Throughout the town posters advertise the County Wicklow gardens festival of Ireland which is in full bloom. It runs until the 30th of June when people are allowed in to private gardens to inspect the horticultural gems. County Wicklow is known for its colourful gardens in which a wide diversity of plants thrive. 'Ecological tourism' is the buzz phrase here with visitors being encouraged to take some of the organized walking tours in the area, or walk the inland Wicklow Way.

From Arklow a sandy beach runs up to Pennycomequick Bridge. I turn right at the Wheely Pump Corner and take up a position on the coastal route to Wicklow town. In the garden of a house, behind a wall, a man stands on a ladder spraying the blossoms on pear trees. He says if I wait for twenty minutes he'll be going to Wicklow to visit his daughter. Sure enough about half an hour later my pear man pulls his Escort out of the driveway and takes me the fifteen miles to Wicklow. When I tell him I'm on an anticlockwise hitchhike of the country on small coastal roads, and that I refuse to take buses or trains, he says he always thought northerners were a contrary and obtuse lot. I have now confirmed it for him.

Wicklow is the county town and stands on the slopes of Ballyguile Hill. It overlooks a wide bay fringed by a crescent curve of coast. The name is a corruption of *Wyking alo*, or Viking meadow and I read to my horror in the guide that the old town of narrow streets has been extensively modernized in recent times.

The pear man drops me beside a tennis club. It is now late afternoon. I wish to reach either Greystones or Bray by the evening. A speedy lift takes me the two miles out of town to Rathnew from where a self-employed plasterer brings me the sixteen miles to Greystones. He has been working on a new pub in Wicklow which the owner wants completed as soon as possible. At present he is working seven days a week but he says the money is good and work is scarce.

Greystones is a dormitory town for Dubliners. It takes its name from a large group of rocks sticking out in the sea south of the harbour – the grey stones. Many Dubliners come to retire in this genteel seaside resort which is regarded as being more sedate than its neighbour, 'brash Bray.' It is surprising therefore to find the town papered with posters advertising a rock concert, 'The Midsummer Rave-Up,' being held over the weekend. The 'summer solstice spectacle' includes in its all-star line up Engine Alley, Alewishus Phontains, Hank Halfhead and the Rambling Turkeys, Four Idle Hands, the Bee Keepers and Jan Roots.

I elect to berth myself here for the night on the basis that there should be some lively Saturday evening entertainment and I am within easy striking distance of Dublin. After dining in the Hungry Monk restaurant where the dessert 'death by chocolate' nearly finishes me off, I wander along the harbour front in pursuit of boating details around Dublin. The hues in the evening sky are a mixture of blue, white, grey and pink. The clouds are ranged as though in opposing factions against each other in long arrow-like shapes. I watch them moving for a time. The sky is turning into a theatrical formation of swirling clouds and peculiar shapes. Behind it all the sun sinks over the peaks of Little Sugar Loaf and Great Sugar Loaf.

The drinkers in the Beach House Bar and members of the yacht club aren't interested in the drama in the sky on their doorstep. They're more concerned about the quality of their beer and beefsteak at the annual barbecue. Across the road from the Beach House the bar of La Touche Hotel attracts a wide social mix. It is heaving with yuppies, yachties, dinkies (double income, no kids), jollies (jet-setting oldies with lots of lolly), yaks (young, adventurous, keen and single), dumbos (drunken, upper-class, middle-aged businessmen over the limit) and a sexy selection of sinbads (single income, no boyfriend and desperate). Fishermen stand shoulder to shoulder with students, tennis players, Hooray Henries and Henriettas, Half Hankhead fans and ordinary Greystoneites.

La Touche is one of those old hotels that has stood the test of time and is enjoying a busy resurgence. Old photographs show the building as it looked when it was known as The Grand. The stones to build it were brought in by sailing ships from Devon. A couple of maps illustrate the close connection between this area and the Welsh coast. The full girth of Cardigan Bay is detailed and on this side the size of Dublin Bay is apparent.

One of the barmen directs me to the receptionist who he says will be able to answer any enquiries about a boat around the bay. The girl behind the desk knows her job well. She also knows Greystones. She says it used to be called 'little Belfast' in the 1940s and 1950s because of the large number of Church of Ireland and Presbyterians living in it. In fact there wasn't even a police station in those days as there was no crime. The present one is open only in the afternoons.

La Touche, she says, were a family of French Huguenot stock. They were pioneers of banking in Ireland and in the middle of the eighteenth century bought most of the land around Greystones. They were also responsible for the development of the town during the railway age. She searches through her contacts book and comes up with the name of a man called Dick Phillips. She says he is a member of a yacht club in Dun Laoghaire and gives me his home telephone number. After an explanation of my trip Dick says he is fairly sure he will be taking part in the Liffey event. He says if I turn up at the west pier in Dun Laoghaire at eleven-thirty he will take me on his boat. It should be reasonably easy, he reckons, to transfer boats at the Liffey and hop on another going to the north side of Dublin.

* * * * *

I rise early on Sunday morning. On no account can I afford to be late for one of the most crucial lifts of the journey. Greystones to Dun Laoghaire is about twelve miles, but because previous Sunday mornings on the road have proved quiet I allow myself two hours to get there. I needn't have worried. A Dublin man, who'd spent the night in Greystones to escape from the noise of the city, is on his way back into the centre and picks me up after a twenty minute wait on the Bray Road.

He likes Greystones but believes it has developed at an alarming rate and is now almost out of control. He is less than kind about the influx of people who've come to live in the area over the years.

'I remember when it was being built-up in the sixties. They searched all over for people to come and live here. They say they not only searched County Wicklow and County Dublin, as well as the island of Ireland, but also the British Isles and everywhere they could, for the scum of the world came to live in Greystones.'

We drive through Bray, Shankill and Killiney, along what is locally known as the 'Bay of Naples.' We pass through Dalkey and arrive in Dun Laoghaire in good time. The town is a busy ferry terminus. The west and east piers, both over a mile long, form a horseshoe and shelter the harbour where scores of yachts and small craft are tied up. For over a hundred and

fifty years a regular ferry service has operated across the sixty-four miles
between Dun Laoghaire and Holyhead in Wales. The port claims to have
the largest passenger throughput in Ireland with over a million people a
year using it.

When I arrive at Dun Laoghaire Motor Yacht Club (DMYC) the
members are preparing for the trip. The event is called a cruise-in-
company and involves several hundred craft coming together and meeting
at the Liffey to raise money for the Society of St. Vincent de Paul. It is part
of the Dublin European City of Culture celebrations.

I make enquiries for Dick Phillips and a man tells me he has gone out in
his boat to test the engine and should be back shortly. The harbour is
buzzing with activity. A leaflet about the cruise says it promises to be the
most spectacular sail ever up the Liffey. The flotilla will make its way to
the Talbot Memorial Bridge where the flagship of the Irish Navy, the *L.E.
Eithne,* will be moored halfway up the river. The leaflet says fancy dress is
to be worn by the crews, and all craft are asked to dress up as well.

I can hardly believe my eyes when I meet Dick and see the luxurious
motor boat in which I am to be taken around Dublin Bay. It would
certainly not be out of place in the Bay of Naples. It is a forty-three foot
power cruiser called *KOTI* and sleeps up to eight people. There is a crew of
four, plus me. Dick's right hand man, Jack Gallagher, shows me round and
explains some nautical terms.

He enlightens me on the meaning of several morse signal codes. The
ones I will need to know, he says, are:

– – –	man overboard
• – – –	I am on fire, keep clear
• • •	my engines are going astern

Very reassuring for a sailing newcomer like me. Jack laughs. When I
telephoned Dick last night I jokingly remarked that I would be prepared to
work my passage. It is therefore not a complete surprise when Jack thrusts
a mop at me and clarifies my deckhand duties. My job involves throwing
water over the deck every so often and brushing it with the mop to keep it
clean. I suppose as jobs go it could be worse.

Before we join the flotilla sailing up-river Dick takes me on a tour of
Dublin Bay. We go out to Dalkey Island, and pass the Muglins where
seagulls squabble over scraps. Across the other side, where I hope to be
going in the afternoon, a large white cloud hangs over Howth Head.

Jack says the people in the DMYC are the friendliest of all the four
yacht clubs in Dun Laoghaire. He says the clubs all are recognized for
different qualities. The Motor Yacht Club are known as slobs; the Na-

tional Club members are called yobs; the people in the Royal St. George are snobs and the members of the Royal Irish are known as nobs.

As we head into the wider stretch of the bay, Dick opens up the *KOTI*. We move smoothly across at twenty-five knots. The bay is crowded with other vessels. Dick says the sea is a 'bit lumpy' but he describes the conditions overall as good.

We enter the Liffey port side and join a colourful and noisy flotilla. Surrounding us are stately vessels of all shapes and sizes: yachts, motor cruisers, racing boats, ketches, catamarans, luggers, sloops, rowing boats and hookers. Even the City of Dublin and Howth lifeboats have joined in the party. They're all vying for space in the congested fairways. A warning comes across on Dick's radio to keep the lanes clear until the *Lady of Mann*, the Isle of Man Steam Packet Company ferry, leaves the harbour.

On our way upstream we pass Poolbeg power station and enter the Dublin Port Authority area where a variety of container vessels, cargo ships and bulk tankers are tied up. A stretch along the front contains mills, warehouses and timber yards until we reach the toll bridge at the Point Depot theatre.

Although it is not a race, there is, I discover amongst sailors and boat owners a certain oneupmanship and pride at stake as to who can get there first. The high jinks though really begin when we arrive at the Talbot Memorial Bridge. The whole raggle-taggle assembly turns into a cacophony of sound. A bellowing of foghorns, klaxons, acoustic horns and whistles greet us as we tie up near the *L.E. Eithne*. The craft arrive, bedecked in balloons, bunting and flags. The Lord Mayor of Dublin, who is the Admiral of the Port, takes the salute as the boats tie up. Dick is an experienced helmsman and easily slots into his allotted position at the Sir John Rogerson's Quay. Soon another five boats tie up alongside the *KOTI*. A party gets underway and bands and dancers on board the Irish Navy vessel entertain the crowds which have turned up to see the craft. The crews throw bags of water at each other as the afternoon degenerates into a frenzy of laughter, wine-drinking, singing and eating. Sailors stumble from boat to boat and from party to party. The cheering, jeering and clapping gets louder. Notes are compared with other boats and noses are turned up at the smaller vessels on display.

My plan is to jump ship on to the *Canterbury* which has agreed to take me. However, unknown to me while I'm downstairs retrieving my ruck, the boat slips away early from her moorings leaving me stranded on the *KOTI* and the prospect of a return trip to Dun Laoghaire.

I jump off and run down the quay but the *Canterbury* has gone. Its crew wave back at me. In a despairing act I shout to another crew berthed beside the quay in a small boat called *First Tri*. Yes, according to a female member of the crew they are going to Howth. There are no steps down to the vessel so I'm forced to abseil down a rope clinging as tight as possible with my feet to the wall. To loud cheers from the crews I scramble on board. We head north out of the bay past Dollymount strand on the way to Howth Head. Further out is the causeway of Bull Island, a *mecca* in the winter for brent geese from Greenland. Throughout the winter thousands of geese, ducks and waders make their home on the island. In 1931 it became the first official bird sanctuary in Ireland, and Dublin Bay is now one of the most important wetland areas in the country.

The crew of the *First Tri* want me to gain some seamanship experience so the skipper, Pat, allows me to take the tiller for a while. The boat is flying twelve coloured pennants which in international sailing language spells out 'DUBLIN'S GREAT.'

En route Pat points out features of the coastline. We pass Doldrum Bay which he says has a Hippy Hole and Lions Head areas. It leads to Dungriffan promontory on which the Baily Lighthouse is situated. Past the lighthouse we come to the high cliffs of Howth Head, home to hundreds of shags, cormorants and other seabirds. Their nesting places have fanciful names such as Gaskins Leap, Highgroom Bed and Pipers Gut. Having negotiated the Nose of Howth, we pass near to Lambay Island and the jagged rocks of Ireland's Eye, which Pat says is often visited by day trippers from Howth. Pat also tells me the coast road around Howth is known as 'the string of pearls' because of the bright glitter of the lights along it after dark. He says it is best seen from the water at night.

On the way into Howth harbour the *First Tri* makes a clean berth unlike the *Lady of Bahia* which runs aground trying to negotiate the entrance into the marina. The boat, which was the lead vessel, is damaged with a hole and is to be beached for the night. The crew and passengers, who looked as if they'd been having a decent party, were brought off by another boat.

In the Howth Yacht Club the members discuss the day's activities, culminating in the drama on their doorstep. This is a club with a proud tradition. The *Howth Seventeens*, the seventeen-foot gaff-rigged sailing boats – most of them originals – are still raced here on Saturdays throughout the summer. They are believed to be the world's oldest surviving one-design class still actively racing under their original rig.

Gazing out through the window across the boats and into the harbour from the bar of the club the *Lady of Bahia* represents a pitiful sight. I mull over the events of the day. I haven't covered a big distance; maybe twenty nautical miles, but I managed to avoid Dublin and saw the city from a new perspective. I met a host of warm and generous people such as Dick Phillips whose hospitality was unsurpassed. Jack Gallagher told me I was the adventurous type like him and he wants me to go with him on a trip to the Arctic Circle on a boat called *Star Wars*. Ruane, a crew member of *First Tri*, is anxious that I accompany him on a motorbike ride through the States to Alaska taking ferry trips across portions of water in America which is his love.

At midnight the club closes and we go our separate ways. Before falling asleep in my guest house I study the map. From the Howth peninsula it should be an easy start north in the morning along the coast of County Dublin and Meath . . . as for the Arctic? . . . I think I'll leave that for another year.

A LIFE-SAVING LOTTO CATCH

Howth to Portaferry

The rumble of the Dublin Area Rapid Transit train – familiarly known as the DART, and which is said stands for 'Delays Are Really Trendy' – disturbs my sleep at seven-thirty and reminds me of my suburban situation. Today's hitching will initially bring me through suburbs and then along the coastal sections of Meath and Louth.

After breakfast a short refreshing walk from Howth to Sutton Cross puts me on the road for Portmarnock and Malahide. A lift with a man working in the corporate entertainment industry, Michael Lynch, takes me through the north Dublin area to Swords. Michael says this area is dubbed Silicon Valley because of the large number of computer and hi-tech industries centred here. It is the location for firms making chemicals, computers and pharmaceuticals and is one of the main industrial bases on Dublin's periphery. Swords, he says, has grown from several thousand in the 1950s to its present population of over thirty thousand.

Two lifts, one with a roofing contractor and the other with a van driver from Nationwide Express Deliveries, bring me the fifteen miles through Lusk, Rush and over to Skerries.

This resort, with its tree-lined street, has a homely feel to it. The woman in the tourist information point, which is housed in the community centre, says they are loosely connected to *Bord Fáilte* but prefer doing their own thing. In the tidy towns report of 1982 the tourist board said Skerries was potentially a pleasant town with lots of charm and character.

The crescent shaped beach is scattered with shingle, seaweed, stones, crisp wrappers and lemonade cans. A section of it, known as 'The Oven,' is a sunny spot on the South Strand between the Sailing Club and the shelters under the Martello Tower.

Out to sea sit St. Patrick's Island, Colt Island and Shenick Island. Near the headland is Peggy's Rock which is shaped like an armchair, and which my guidebook says was sometimes called the Pony Rock because when it was uncovered a pony could safely cross to Shenick. A host of charming place names are linked with Skerries. There is Tinkers Lane, Guttery Lane and Featherbed Lane. 'The Crack' is a short cut from Lower Strand Street down to Harbour Road. 'Grey Mare' is a group of large rocks at the back of the harbour. The greyish colour is a result of the seagull's droppings.

The outline on my map of County Meath bears a striking resemblance to the shape of France. The area which concerns me is a short section to the east sticking out like an arm touching the sea. The county booklet says Meath has a wealth of historic sites with medieval castles, churches and monuments, including Newgrange, the Hill of Tara, Navan and Trim Castle. One of the main sporting events in the area appears to be an ecclesiastical horse race. The international 'Nun Run' as it is known, is a horse-race confined to nuns, and is held every summer in a field within sight of Trim Castle. The guide says there is never any shortage of sisters willing to gallop around the course at break-neck speed for prizemoney which they donate to charity.

From Skerries my lift with Richard Hurley brings me through Balbriggan across the River Slane into County Meath and up to Drogheda. I've no wish to hang around Drogheda and am anxious to try to get along the Louth coast and then aim for a lift around the Cooley peninsula. Drogheda marks my entry into Louth, the smallest county in Ireland, with three hundred and seventeen square miles.

The trip out to the sea from Drogheda takes me along the Newfoundwell Road where posters on telegraph poles call for action to 'repair our awful roads.' The man who picks me up says drivers need a PhD when they're negotiating the roads around the area. This doesn't mean a Doctor of Philosophy degree but in fact stands for experience in pothole dodging. He says some of the roads in the area are almost craterised and have attracted wild animals. He has a theory the councils are deliberately using sub-standard building materials in the roads.

He can't understand why I should want to go to Clogher Head and says it will be difficult hitching from there. I tell him it's a place I've never visited and I want to have a look at how the fishing industry is faring in the area. He says the village has gone steadily down hill from the 1960s when people from Northern Ireland moved into the caravan sites!

When I get to Clogher Head I meet a fisherman called Thomas Molloy who is not happy with his lot. He says fishermen are reaping from the sea all the time but are not sowing.

'We can't keep taking from nature without putting something back. The industry here is bordering on the critical. Every day there are fewer fish in the Irish Sea and, in any case, it is grossly overfished.'

In Clogher Head, he says, the boats mainly fish for prawns and in any single night there could be up to one hundred heading out to sea. They also fish for plaice, cod and monkfish. Boats come from Skerries, Balbriggan and Kilkeel in County Down to fish here and they go out as far as Whitehaven on the Cumbrian coast. Thomas says because the boats are bigger than ever they can go much further.

'The problem is that prawns don't drop out of the sky and there is a limit to everything. Nothing goes on for ever. The bigger boats are towing two nets while fishing, and are doubling the amount they catch. They are so expensive to operate that if they don't fish with two nets they could not survive.'

Thomas sees the solution coming from the imposition of limits of a few miles. 'No fishing should be allowed within five miles for at least two or three years along the east coast and within a few years I think that will be introduced by the authorities. Restrictions are inevitable, but the biggest hurdle will be enforcing them. If the fishing industry collapsed it would mean more emigration as there is nothing else for people here.'

He says Clogher Head has always been a closely knit fishing community and there is no other way of life for the locals. Not many people, he observes, are willing to speak about the situation or to face up to realities.

Thomas talks about Clogher Head as a place to visit. He says many people feel it has a certain sourness about it. 'It had a reputation as a rough sort of place in the past, and fights in the bars were a frequent occurrence. But when you get to know the people here it could be one of the best places anywhere along the coast and the locals are friendly once they know you. When they adjust to you it is fine, but that can take some time and they don't, by and large, get many outsiders coming to settle here.'

He asks me some questions about my trip, trying to get me to draw comparisons with other fishing towns around the coast. I tell him his opinions are the most candid I've heard, although similar views have been echoed elsewhere.

I head off in search of a telephone. In Sharkey's pub an antiquated black device with A and B buttons hangs on the wall. I wish to get through to a contact in Carlingford. In the words of the song I'm trying to 'find me a handy boatman' to take me across the lough into County Down either tonight or in the morning. It is one of those telephones which has slots for one penny, two pence and five pence pieces – somewhat incongruous as the cheapest call is thirty pence. I lose ninety pence in coins by failing to push the right buttons and being cut off several times. After a row with the operator, who doesn't seem to understand English, I finally get through. I arrange to ring a man called Peadar Ellmore when I reach Carlingford.

The main street of Clogher Head is a sad somnolent affair on this cold windy Monday afternoon. Six of the village's eight pubs are closed. The credit union is shut, and with the exception of two cars, the beach and caravan parks are empty. Reilly and Sharkey seem to be the names that run the place. The man in the grocery shop says the tourist season has not yet begun in earnest. He tells me there is no point in trying to hitch up to Annagassan as there is little or no traffic and people would not give lifts to strangers. The postmistress says they don't have a tourist office as there is no need for one. Clogher Head is one of those places that never really sniffs many tourists. The German campervans have not penetrated this far north and you would be hard pushed to see why they should want to come.

Walking up the hill towards the end of main street I feel conspicuous and out of place with my rucksack. Nothing is stirring. There is an eerie stillness. Half a dozen parked cars, all with LH plates signifying local registrations from County Louth, sit along main street. The mood is forbidding. It is the quietest and most desolate coastal place of my trip. The grocer had said my best bet was to try to get a lift into Dunleer which would bring me back to the main road and on to Dundalk through Castlebellingham. He said there will be some traffic when the fish process-ing factory workers finish their shifts at five o'clock. It is now three thirty-five. Not for the first time, I have a long wait ahead.

Clogher Head doesn't reveal too many secrets. But I feel eyes; eyes watching me. I get the impression of being looked at from behind lace curtains and of people surreptitiously stealing glances through windows, yet I never see anybody. I just have an uncomfortable feeling about the place. It's the first time anywhere that I have never felt truly at home. Two young women walk past me with their arms folded like a pair of old maidens and look through me. An older woman gives me a steely gaze and crosses the street. In any other street, in any other village, in any other county on my travels they would have at least passed the time of day, made a casual remark about the weather or nodded their heads. Here there is not even a tiny nod. They do not seem interested in any outsider's presence. Even the dogs are not curious about me; a Yorkshire terrier lies sleeping across the street stretched out in a doorway.

Motorists have no interest in hitchhikers either. During the first half hour three cars pass. The drivers all give me suspicious looks. I walk back into the village to see if there is any sign of movement or if there is a chance of catching a delivery man on his way home. But it is too late in the day. I have missed them, if they ever came here at all.

On the way back to my hitching spot a drunk stumbles out of the Sail Inn and trips over the sleeping terrier. Another couple of cars pass me. I begin to despair and a sense of helpless frustration creeps over me. I consider surrendering, giving myself up, going to the police for help, or simply looking for a taxi or bus. I'm only about sixty miles from home, although the way I wish to go by the coastal route will mean about one hundred and fifty miles. The time is approaching five o'clock. My spirits lift slightly when half a dozen cars appear. They gather speed as they drive past me without so much as an acknowledgement. At this rate I may be lucky to reach Carlingford by darkness.

The day is eventually saved by a Belfast man and his wife who're on a drive through the area for old time's sake. Vinny McCann says they used to come here in the sixties when it was a popular place. This is the first time they've been back. They are not impressed.

'I don't think we'll ever come back here for a holiday,' he says. 'We just wanted to see how it had changed over the years and decided to come for a drive. We also wanted to cross the border to buy our lotto tickets in Dundalk on the way through.'

Lucky for me, otherwise I could have spent the rest of the evening standing at one end of the main street. We soon come to Dundalk. 'El Paso' as it is known to journalists is full of pubs which are in turn normally full of *desperadoes* or rogues. This evening though it looks remarkably absent of fugitives, and resembles any similar Irish town I've passed through with people quietly going about their business. Dundalk is an administrative centre and stopping off place in the journey between Belfast and Dublin. Vinny and his wife are on their way back to Belfast. Would I like a lift? A short pause. No, I have some unfinished business to attend to along the coast. They drop me two miles outside Dundalk at the turnoff for the Cooley peninsula where I'm picked up within five minutes.

Leslie Adamson is on his way home to Carlingford. He says he used to repair radios and television sets in the days when all that could go wrong was the valve.

'The age of the microchip put me out of business, and I decided to leave it to the younger men who are well qualified and up to date on the new technology. What I most disliked about the job was that it was seven days a week. You never had a day off, or rarely an hour or two to yourself. People would call at the house on Sunday afternoons and say their mother's television set had blown up and could I come immediately and fix it as her favourite programme is coming on.'

The Cooley peninsula is described as a land of myth, legend and fun. In

Viking times Carlingford was an important place and it enjoyed a rejuve-
nation under the Anglo-Normans. The Coat of Arms of 1720 symbolizes
its Viking and Norman history and its importance as a centre of commerce. Locals say the profile of Finn MacCool, lying at rest, is outlined on
Carlingford Mountain. Unfortunately this is not apparent tonight as the
mountain is enveloped in cloud. Across the lough the mountains of
Mourne are also clouded over.

    After finding a guest house I set about establishing contact with Peadar
Ellmore. He comes into town to meet me and agrees to take me across the
lough in the morning to Greencastle in County Down – 'weather permitting.' That chilling phrase, I tell him, has become my watchword throughout the trip.

                                    * * * * *

The next morning Peadar and the *Queen Maeve* are waiting for me when I
arrive at the quay at half past eight. A thin whispy veneer of mist is
covering Slieve Foye on the Carlingford side and the clouds look as if they
have never moved from yesterday's position over the Mourne peaks. This
view is more akin to the west coast of Ireland than the east and for a
moment I imagine I am in Mayo or Galway.

    Peadar says when Finn MacCool has his cap on you must put your coat
on as it is sure to be cold. This morning though the lough is calm and it
should be a reasonably straightforward crossing but he says he may have to
do some 'rock-dodging' here and there. He keeps out of the navigational
channel as there is a strong current in places. Peadar is an experienced
sailor and takes the helm with confidence having made this crossing
countless times.

    Like yesterday in Clogher Head I feel eyes watching me again. This
time it is a British naval patrol boat keeping an eye on us as we enter
Northern Ireland waters. I keep an eye on it with my binoculars and a
hand appears from nowhere to give me a wave. We travel at five knots
across the lough's smooth surface and Peadar points out Haulbowline
Lighthouse on an island at the entrance to the lough. He keeps his sights
on it as it's a good guide. We pass near the port of Greenore, avoiding the
run of tide which can sometimes be tricky. Peadar grew up in the area and
is familiar with the whole peninsula. He says Green Island in the lough
had a big colony of roseate terns for many years. In the early seventies
there were more than six hundred pairs, and although their numbers have
substantially decreased some are still to be seen in the Greencastle area.

    One of the most popular forms of recreation is hiring sea fishing boats
and the lough is noted for spurdog, conger, cod and mackerel. Peadar says

the area around Omeath is known for its musical townland names. 'There is a poem or song, I believe, dealing with the ten townlands of Omeath and although I don't know it I remember all the names of the townlands,' he says. He runs through them:

Ballyonan, Ballintesken and Knocknagoran; Drumlagh, Lislea and Cornamuckla; Ardaghy, Bavan, Tullagh and Corrakett.

With practised ease Peadar pulls up in under an hour at Cunningham's Pier in Greencastle and I set foot on northern soil for the first time in over three weeks. He says he can sort out a lift for me with Leo Cunningham who operates the pilot boat in Carlingford Lough. The clouds have lifted to reveal my first glimpse of Slieve Donard and the Mourne Mountains. It dawns on me that I am at last near home. From here I need to get to Kilkeel, around the side of Dundrum Bay and up to Strangford, then over to the Ards peninsula and along the coast of north Down back into Belfast. It's a distance of almost a hundred miles and it's unlikely I'll be able to complete it in one day.

Leo Cunningham and his brother, Sean, are self-employed lock pilots. Their job is an important one as the lough is awkward in some places for shipping. It involves meeting the vessels at the entrance, going on board and guiding them to whichever port they are heading. Leo says they have become used to dealing with the full spectrum of foreign shipping: paper from Finland, timber from Canada, coal from Rotterdam, steel from Spain and fertilizer from France. The main ports which the ships head for are Warrenpoint on the County Down side and Greenore on the Cooley peninsula.

Leo drops me in the centre of Kilkeel with its newly painted red, white and blue kerbstones and bunting much in evidence for the twelfth of July parade in a few weeks' time. Kilkeel has the bustle of a busy fishing town. I immediately notice how the accent in this area is strikingly reminiscent of the Scottish dialect. The woman in the cafe in Greencastle Street warns me that my cup might '*cowp*' over if I don't put it on the right size of saucer.

The bridge over the Aughrim River leads through the town and I make my way down Rooney Road to the harbour. My purpose is twofold: to meet the harbour master in charge of one of Ireland's busiest fishing ports, and then seek out the weigh master.

Sam Hanna is an affable harbour master. He gives me a potted present-day account of the fishing in the area. Kilkeel harbour, he says, is home to one hundred and twenty-five boats over forty feet and twenty under that. Forty per cent fish for prawns and about forty per cent are involved in what he calls bottom or mid-water trawling.

'It is known as a pelagic trawl,' Sam explains. 'That is a trawl involving fishing anywhere between the surface or bottom at any time of the day or night.

'The boats from Kilkeel work in an area stretching from the Bay of Biscay to the north of Scotland. They work for mackerel, herrings and some commercial fish such as blue whiting.'

Sam agrees that the Irish Sea is overfished. 'The only way around it is the quotas which are enforced from Brussels. We have to work hard at the conservation of fish and there are constant scientific studies going on. Of course this doesn't please the fishermen all the time, but it is beginning to have an impact in some areas and is working. We have found the position is being stabilized in certain areas, although not in the Irish Sea yet.'

From Kilkeel the fish are distributed throughout Britain and Europe. 'Our fish go from here to Manchester market or down to Billingsgate. We also export to Spain, France, Italy and Germany. A lot of the highest quality fish is for the continental market. We have a few crabs and lobster but that is a precarious market although it is sometimes quite good in July and August.'

Looking to the future of the industry in the nineties Sam says it is difficult to prophesy what will happen.

'If we are to survive into the twenty-first century there must be strict conservation and it must be enforced properly. This is the crucial area. If it continues as it did in the seventies and eighties it could peter out and the consequences would be disastrous as the town employs so many people connected with the fish business.

'It is not only the fishermen's families who will be affected, but also the fish processing workers, the salesmen, lorry drivers and the large number of others engaged in the industry.'

I make a final request of Sam before leaving. I wish to use one of the weighbridges in the harbour to find out how much I've been carrying around on my back for the past twenty-six days.

In the shed of S.R. Donnan, wholesale fish merchants, the weigh master throws the paraphernalia of my trip on to the scales. It weighs twenty-four pounds or eleven kilos. He tells me that in Kilkeel fish terms I've been carrying the equivalent of a stone and three-quarter of prawns. He laughs heartily and says that after twenty-six days there would have been an almighty pong.

From Kilkeel I hitch a lift after half an hour with a firm of cross channel hauliers from Kells in County Antrim. Greg Montgomery is on a delivery to Newcastle and runs me along the coastal route through Annalong and Glassdrumman into the main street. Inland the Mourne Mountains lie to our left and look their finest in the afternoon sun.

Newcastle (with a population of 7,500) is, like so many places I've passed through, crammed with families. The town is dominated by the mountains and the main industry is tourism. In many ways, because of the mountains on its doorstep, it is a much more enchanting holiday town than places such as Portrush, Ballybunion or Tramore. From the main street you look up at what could almost be an Alpine view. The town has its share of amusement arcades but they are quieter and more discreet compared with those I've come across in other resorts. The influence of the nearby fresh mountain air must have something to do with it.

The area used to be known as Ballaghbeg – *Bealach Beg* – 'the little road.' In 1588 the name of Newcastle was taken from the castle erected just south of the Shimna River. By the 1830s the town started to develop as a seaside resort and it became known as the queen of northern bathing places. Part of the town still has its Victorian character with seaside villas and terraces. It stretches around the curve of Dundrum Bay, and from the promenade the full extent of the bay can be seen from St. John's Point to where the mountains collide with the sea.

From the roundabout on the Belfast road I'm in search of a lift to take me to Clough and then wish to swing down through the Lecale peninsula. Beside me loom the mountains with the dominant peak, Slieve Donard, standing out clear. At two thousand seven hundred and ninety-six feet it towers over the town. Donard – which is the highest peak in Ulster – was acquired by the National Trust early in 1991. I scout the empty hills with my binoculars. During the week these mountains must be one of the most under-used assets anywhere in the island of Ireland.

The man who picks me up knows them better than most. Steve Synnott is an outdoor pursuits instructor and works at Shannaghmore, an outdoor education centre in the Mournes. He regularly takes weekend orienteering courses and brings school groups and youth clubs for treks through the hills. He is a man with a passion for the mountains. Even on his days off he says he heads into the hills for a hike. I tell him his would be my ideal type of job, but of course there's more to it than taking in fresh air and chasing girl guides through forest parks.

'The Mournes are a wonderful natural resource and although you get quite a few groups out at the weekends they are generally deserted during the week,' he says. 'The high Mournes, that is the central range from Donard over to Bingian are the most popular, but many people never venture into the western part which is the range on the other side of the Spelga Pass. It includes Pigeon Rock, Eagle Mountain and Slievemoughanmore and represents some very exciting rambling.'

It's an important lift with Steve. He takes me out of Newcastle, through Dundrum and sets me on the Blackstaff Road in Clough. Two lifts – one from a music teacher on his way to take a piano lesson in Killough, and the other from a local publican – bring me to Ardglass.

My hitching spot from here affords views of a dense flock of black-headed gulls and oystercatchers crouched on the roofs of sheds and on the sea front. A black cat has found a small bird lying in rocks near the harbour. It sees me watching it and, before slinking off, gives me a long stare that says it has been caught red-handed.

Within ten minutes I'm picked up by a young man, who doesn't look as if he's old enough to control a BMX bicycle never mind the BMW that he clearly doesn't own. His name is Andrew and he says he is going to 'Strankford.' Andrew had been asked to return the car by a friend who had borrowed it from someone else last night in what appears to be a complicated arrangement.

The name Strangford means 'strong-flowing fiord.' It comes from the Vikings who, during their raids, were aware of the strength of the tidal currents at the mouth of the *fiord*. The town developed much of its present appearance early in the seventeenth century and some of the buildings have their origins in this period. The remains of the castle stand overlooking the centre of the town and there is a Georgian feel to the place.

A number of buildings in the centre are listed for their special architectural or historic interest and the town has been designated a conservation area. Many of the houses have a fine stone finish with intricate brick detailing – the sort of thing found in the lowlands of Scotland. Tiers of buildings lead down to the small harbour where the regular ferry service links the town with Portaferry on the Ards peninsula. Boats leave each terminal at half-hourly intervals in the summer and ply across the narrow channel at the entrance to the lough from early morning until late evening.

My ride on the MV *Strangford* takes about ten minutes. It also launches me on the final leg of my journey, though the analogy with that particular limb is not quite appropriate as the Ards peninsula resembles something more akin to an arm. It stretches out from under Belfast Lough at Bangor and Donaghadee and falls down to enclose the lough as though offering much needed protection from the wild rage of the sea.

The ferry has room for about twenty vehicles and on this trip carries five cars and two vans with a few pedestrians. As the vessel slips from the harbour a salty spray shoots up from the ripple of water and dampens the back of my head. We swing past Swan Island which is the nesting place for gulls and terns. The main occupants are black-headed gulls which flap over from the island and circle low over the ferry. They return to sit on their nests among clumps of grass. Swan Island is just one of a hundred or so in Strangford Lough, the largest sea inlet in the British Isles.

As we glide across, the long line of white and pale coloured two storey buildings on the water front of Portaferry loom larger by the minute. In the distance the soft shapes of small rolling hills or drumlins create a tranquil backdrop. With a couple of clanks the ferry docks and the cars, vans and pedestrians file off into the evening sunshine.

After checking into Mrs. Adair's B & B in the centre of the village, I feel in need of a late evening drink to mark my last night on the road. An orange sun is setting over the lough. In the water a cormorant sails past. A grey heron, with its long legs and sinuous neck, steps uncertainly from one lump of seaweed to another, and then pauses to look at a lone dark seal bobbing up and down in the water.

A man in the Slip Inn, from where the harbour wildlife is visible, says some people in Portaferry don't like the heron. There is an old belief here that a heron flying over the house is unlucky. On the wall of the bar a map of Ireland by one Baptista Boazio, and drawn up in 1599, attracts my interest. It is said to be the first ever map of Ireland. I study it for several minutes and retrace my route around the coast to reassure myself that I really have done it. I muse over the names which existed in those days and see where I would have gone four hundred years ago – had there been any cars along the coast of *Irlandiae*.

Starting from *Knockfergus*, I pass through Sorleyboye and O'Donnell's contrey into *Dongall*. Then through Cos. *Slego* and Mayo and around the *Baie of Galwaie* into Co. Clare. From there my finger runs along the Co. *Kiry* coast, the *Baie of Dingle* past *Beare*, *Flu Bantre*, and into Co. *Corke*; along the *Baie of Kinfale* to *Yogholl* and across to Co. *Waterforde*. Then up the east coast through Cos. *Wexforde*, Wicklow, the *Baie of Dublin* to the Head of *Houth* and *Skirries*. Onwards to Point *Cloghere*, Carlingford, *GreenCaft* in Co. *Downe*, around *Lecaile* to *Porfere*, along the *Arde* and into *Belfaft*, where I hope to arrive tomorrow.

ALICE CONFRONTS MARITIME BUREAUCRACY

Portaferry to Belfast

Over breakfast I read a folding map and visitors guide to the area. It has been compiled by a diverse number of bodies, all with a common laudable interest, who come under the collective banner of the 'Strangford Lough Interpretative Group.' Their guide murmurs enticingly about the Ards peninsula being surrounded by a necklace of towns and fishing villages each with its own individual character.

The landlady, Mrs. Adair, says there'll be little chance of a lift to Kearney. 'You might get a car every fifteen minutes on that road if you're lucky,' she declares . . . but she adds, 'You should have no problem getting a lift as you don't have long hair and a pony tail like so many of the hitchers on the roads these days.'

I tell her I'm not in any hurry and have all day to get along the coast into Belfast. She shakes her head and fixes me with one of those curious disbelieving looks that I have come to know and understand so well from coastal landladies over the past twenty-seven days.

On the way to Kearney a herd of cattle sit contentedly in the morning sunshine on a mound of grass looking out towards Strangford. They take no interest in the to-ings and fro-ings of the ferry. Behind them in the far distance two Mourne peaks, Donard and Meelmore are clearly visible. The lough is certainly living up to its name this morning with strong-flowing currents.

A local man who says he is a shift worker in Newtownards takes me the four miles to Kearney. He drops me at the turnoff for the village and I walk to a sign which says:

149

*The National Trust, Kearney. No cars beyond this point. All vehicles to
use car park.*

What an ideal village. Probably the only one in Ireland that does not
allow cars in its streets. The Trust acquired the village in 1965. It consists
of thirty-one acres of foreshore and four acres of village land with thirteen
houses and covenants over a further two hundred and eighty-four acres.
Every house is whitewashed and most have black doors and black window
frames. The only sign of life comes from a man cutting the grass on a
mower at one of the houses. He says if I want information about Kearney I
should speak to the warden, Jack Suckling, who lives at the shore front.

Jack looks after the properties for the National Trust which bought the
village with money collected during a coastline campaign called Enterprise Neptune. He tells me there's a colony of seals five hundred yards off
Kearney Point. Over the years their numbers have become depleted but in
the last two years they have been slowly increasing again and they can be
seen basking on rocks at low tide.

He also talks about a wild flower called alexanders which is growing just
outside his house. He believes it was introduced into Britain by the
Romans and although they never came to Ireland the seed made its way
across. There is a theory that it may have been brought over by birds.

'It is a rather insipid plant,' Jack says, pulling off some leaves. 'I believe
it was the forerunner to celery and people used to put it on scones. It was
used as a herb in cooking but is now out of favour.' It flowers in May when
it grows to about four feet. The plant is now past flowering and its yellow
seed heads have faded to brown.

Jack has lived in Kearney for ten years. He says there are only four
permanent residents in the village. The other houses are holiday homes
where people come to stay at weekends or during the summer. As a
working village Kearney does not exist. There are no shops, schools,
doctors, police, pubs or post office. The nearest are in Portaferry or
Cloghy, both four miles away in opposite directions.

From Kearney I rejoin the main Cloghy road and sit on a low wall
waiting for a lift. Behind me are the remains of what looks like a round
tower or mill about twenty feet in height. A blanket of peace and silence
surrounds the area broken only by the lapping waves at Quintin Bay half a
mile along the Portaferry road.

Two men pick me up. They're on their way to Portavogie to hire a crane
for landscape building. Like Killybegs, Castletownbere and Kilmore Quay,
fishing and the sea has been a way of life in Portavogie for many years. Its
fortunes begin and end with the industry. Today it has a large modern
trawler fleet and is noted for its prawns.

The name of the village means '*harbour of the bog*' and at the harbour itself I meet Tom Hughes, the skipper of a seventy-seven foot trawler. I am interested in finding out about the high-technology equipment used by fishermen and Tom brings me on board.

The crew of six is preparing to head off for fishing at Rockall on the west coast of Ireland. They will spend up to ten days at sea. Inside the boat Tom takes me through the details of a bank of screens which line one side of the cabin. It could be the interior of a space mission control station. The familiar paper charts have been replaced by an array of electronic gadgetry which has changed the working lives of modern fishermen.

Besides the radar equipment there is a net transducer which is attached to the fishing net and enables Tom to see the fish being caught. Next to this is a colour video sounder for viewing the fish under the hull of the boat. A paper sounder gives a record of the seabed and any fish seen; there is a video sounder which is used with different frequency for the various types of fish. Two video plotters chart the course – one uses discs and the other cassettes. One works on a small cassette tape and identifies wrecks and under water obstructions to help the crew become familiar with what is on the seabed.

Tom points out his satellite navigators and a Decca navigator which works by signals as a land based grid reference. He uses Loran, a long range navigator for far off use. He also has wireless communication and VHF for contact with other boats. A closed circuit television monitor completes the picture.

Not surprisingly Tom studied electronics for three years and likes to keep up to date with the most advanced fishing techniques. He says his is the only boat with such modern, sophisticated equipment in Portavogie. To fit out and buy a similar boat today would cost about a million pounds.

'Fishing in the nineties is very big business,' Tom says. 'We want to keep ahead of the field but realistically there are too many boats in the sea chasing too few fish. We need to reduce the number of boats.'

He says Britain won't adopt the EC scrapping grant. Under this system the capacity of the fleet would be kept down.

'Britain adopted it once before but big companies with boats on oil rigs brought them back into fishing and claimed grants. They soaked up all the money at that time and there was a lot of corruption. They are putting serious pressure on the fishing fleet. We are supposed to be a common market but our fishermen are suffering because of this. They give you the value of the boat and take away your licence. The theory is that after a certain period of time the fish stock will then increase. But the EC will not give us grants for anything because Britain will not adopt the scrapping grant system.'

In other countries, Tom says, if fishermen wish to re-engine their boats they can do it easily. 'If we want to change our method of fishing to a completely new one of catching different types of fish we used to be able to get a grant but now we can't do that.'

Looking to the future Tom says survival will depend on who is left in the business in a few years' time.

He grumbles about the unfairness of the system. 'Britain has the biggest number of fishery officers, patrol boats and aircraft in the EC and the most fishery officers ashore. They are making bloody sure they are penalizing fishermen very hard. In Spain they get away with murder. They are given all the grants, yet they have the least number of fishery officers and the biggest fleets.'

Tom says some boats in Portavogie are in serious financial trouble with the banks. 'But what can the banks do? They are better off allowing the fishing boats to go out and catch something. If they re-introduced the scrapping grants then the banks would get their money back straight away.'

Local skippers also feel any fishing ban which may be imposed on them for several days will not help conservation efforts as the boats will simply try to catch more fish when they are at sea to make the most of their restricted time.

One other problem Tom has to worry about is submarines which are spotted in the Irish Sea from time to time. 'Fortunately we have never had an incident with them, but I know some trawlermen who have, and it can be a terrifying experience,' he says.

'The submarines are from the American base on the Clyde and have come pretty close to us on occasions. We see them on the surface maybe once a month, but we don't know how many there are travelling up and down the sea. It is certainly a worry for us all.'

As I take my leave from Tom I reflect on the fisherman's life: quotas, patrol boats, fishery officers, heavy competition, scarcity of fish, pollution, bad weather, submarines . . . what an existence to have to contend with that lot each working day.

* * * * *

I haven't even walked out of Portavogie when Jeff Savage stops to pick me up. He is a housing executive grants officer and is on his way to Donaghadee, fifteen miles along the peninsula.

Jeff says Savage is a common name in the area. After John de Courcy conquered Ulster in 1177 he gave many acres of Down to his retainers and Kearney fell to the Savages. Their descendants remain in Portaferry until the present day. Jeff, who's interested in the history of the clan, says the telephone directory lists about two hundred; most live in County Down. It is also a common name in the Republic, especially in the Munster area, around Cork and Limerick.

Jeff says he's not sure if he wants to be able to trace his ancestry back to a certain Sir Robert Savage. Before going into battle with the Irish, Sir Robert prepared a supper, which was to be served to his enemies if they defeated him, or was to be for himself and his friends if he returned victorious. On that day he slew three thousand Irishmen and returned thanking God for his success to eat his supper. He is also reputed to have given each man in his army a draft of *usquebaugh* (whiskey) before the battle.

'When you hear stories like that it is no wonder that the name means wild or savage,' Jeff says grimly. 'I think the phrase '*Savage by name, Savage by nature*' is appropriate given the family pedigree.' In 1797 the Savages changed their name to Nugent. This led to a saying which became prevalent at the time: '*I'd rather have an old Savage than a new gent*'.

Jeff says the area south of Portavogie along the coast of the peninsula is known as Disneyland.

'It stems from the local *lingua franca*,' he explains. 'The people here are supposed to say they disney know this, or disney know that when they are asked certain questions.'

In Donaghadee I call into Grace Neill's Bar for a lunchtime sandwich. The town was once an important port and was called the 'Dover of Ireland.' For three hundred years a ferry service operated across the twenty-one miles separating Donaghadee and Portpatrick in Scotland. The sailing ships carried horses, sheep, wool, mail and cattle as well as passengers.

Grace Neill's is the oldest pub in Northern Ireland and dates from 1641. A notice on the wall says Peter the Great of Russia is reputed to have stayed here in the eighteenth century on his way to Warrenpoint to study Irish shipbuilding prior to starting the Russian shipbuilding industry. Behind the bar, jars of mussels, cockles, and pickled eggs sit alongside Pig's Nose and Sheep's Dip whisky. The last time I'd seen that variety was at Ballycastle in County Antrim on my first day. It serves to remind me, along with the John de Courcy connection, that I've now almost come the complete circle and need to push quickly on to Bangor.

* * * * *

My final scheme involves a lift the six miles to Bangor from where I hope to find a boat to take me up Belfast Lough into the docks. A quick ride takes me to Bangor where I have a look at the local history scene with a walk around the North Down Heritage Centre. It is based in solid stone buildings which were originally the laundry, stables and stores of Bangor Castle built in 1852. They've now been turned into a centre where the old days of Bangor and its environs live on.

The exhibition rooms take the visitor from the first recorded raid on Bangor Abbey by the Vikings in 810 and its repeated sackings, through the arrival of the Scottish settlers and landed families in the seventeenth century, up to the present day. In a large glass case a model shows a Viking burial at Ballyholme. It was found around 1905 and depicts the crew excavating the grave and paying farewell to their comrades whose resting place lay undisturbed for a thousand years.

Another gallery pronounces itself a theme area of nostalgia for the heyday of north Down as a choice for holidays. There are montages of saucy postcards set alongside old views of the town in the days when seaside was spelt sea-side. Framed and block mounted posters proclaim the '*Renowned Ballroom*' of Caproni's where, in August 1948, the holiday maker could dance nightly to Vic Lewis and his Orchestra.

The Bangor that people come to visit today is a bustling town. It has developed immeasurably from the views captured in the heritage centre. The commercial area is dominated by banks and building societies. I count no fewer than nine along a five hundred yard stretch of both sides of High Street. No doubt the descendants of those canny Scottish settlers are anxious to take care of their hard-earned cash. North Down is in fact known as the 'gold coast' of Northern Ireland, and the air of affluence is apparent around the streets of Bangor.

The spanking new marina though is the centrepiece of attraction. I am now only twelve miles from home. It seems too tame to stand at the side of the road hitching a lift when I could try for a boat. In any case I reckon it will be hard catching a lift into Belfast. The drivers along this road are not noted for their generosity to hitchhikers.

I make my way to the marina and a fisherman gives me the name of Brian Meharg who has just returned from a trip around the harbour with a party of schoolchildren. The time is three o'clock. Brian is willing to take me up Belfast Lough by boat but must return by six o'clock for a herring fishing trip. The journey will take just over an hour each way. Without further ado I climb down into the *Alice Laird*.

She is a twenty-six foot open passenger boat built by a local firm, owned by Jimmy Laird. He built it when he was eighty-four and it was his twelfth vessel named Alice after his wife.

Brian says we need to get clearance from Belfast harbour authority before we can land in the port and he'll do that on the VHF radio on the way in. He says it shouldn't be difficult although some questions may be

asked. We prepare to move off and in the process disturb a dozen guillemots swimming around the boat. Slowly we pull out of Bangor harbour on
my tenth and final aquatic journey – a mere nine nautical miles from
Belfast port.

Brian says Belfast Lough has the busiest shipping lanes in Ireland and
sailors must have their wits about them as one of the most complex tidal
systems in Ireland is in the Copeland Islands area further out to sea.

'There are tides heading towards the Isle of Man and they meet in the
area. It is known as 'Ram Harry' and it is a tidal race where the currents
come together and create an exaggerated surge in the water. A force three
could easily turn into a force six or seven in that area creating heavy
swells.'

Brian reckons the south side of the lough along the north Down coast is
more scenic. He points to both sides of the shore and says the difference is
obvious seen from the lough.

'The north side is ugly. Just look at all the houses built along the shore
front on the Antrim side leading out to the power station. With some
careful planning there has been very little development along the County
Down side and it is mostly parkland and trees. 'I think most people would
agree that County Down has a softer landscape and a gentler appearance
seen from the lough, although I suppose you wouldn't need to say that too
loud in Carrickfergus or Larne.'

As we make our way in we pass Carnalea golf course, Crawfordsburn
country park and Helen's Bay beach, cutting into Grey Point, Rockport
Reef and Craigavad, which is known as '*Dogs of the Rock.*'

Brian calls up Belfast harbour and alerts them of our presence and
proposed arrival at Clarendon Dock. He makes several unsuccessful at-
tempts to contact them on the VHF. Each time the message breaks up and
they don't receive us. When he finally gets through and explains what he
wants a man says he'll come back to him. A few minutes later a voice
crackles over the radio and asks for the message to be repeated. Another
delay. Then the voice says: 'Ah, Roger on that request there. I'm afraid we
cannot permit this drop without prior clearance from the harbour office.'

My heart sinks. Brian goes back on the line again and, to give us time to
plan a course of action, says he could not understand the information. The
message from the man at the harbour is repeated. Loud and clear this time.
The voice is becoming familiar to me. He says if we want to land at
Clarendon Dock we must telephone from a land line.

I feel frustrated. Brian takes it all in his stride and thinks things over. I
tell him I'm not going to be defeated by red tape and bureaucracy at this
late stage with only four miles to go. He knows my resolve is strong and
comes up with a solution. After negotiating shallow water he puts in at the

Royal North of Ireland Yacht Club at Cultra. I jump on to the jetty, run in to telephone the harbour commissioners and make some heart-rending pleading noises to persuade them to change their mind.

I condense my story and explain why and how I have managed to get boats around the cities of Ireland as part of my trip. The conversation continues like this:

HARBOUR BUREAUCRAT: These are the busiest shipping lanes in Ireland and if we allowed you in we could be creating a precedent for other people. You must have prior permission from the harbour office.

TIRED HITCHHIKER: I didn't realize they were so busy, otherwise I would, of course, have written in advance for landing permission.

HARBOUR BUREAUCRAT: There is a vast amount of shipping using this lough. It is the premier port in Ireland and that is why we insist on prior clearance being arranged. We can't just let anybody in because we could be swamped with people.

INGRATIATING HITCHHIKER: I find it hard to believe that you will be inundated with requests each day from hitchhikers wanting to come up Belfast Lough in a boat. In any case as I'm writing about my trip it will help clarify the situation. Naturally I'll point out these are the busiest shipping lanes anywhere in all of Ireland. (In all of the world if you like, I lie to myself).

After more plaintive noises the captain at the other end of the line shows he has a streak of humanity and agrees to bend the rules on this occasion. But just this once. I promise not to make a habit of these type of requests.

I run back down the jetty and Brian pulls up with the *Alice Laird*. I cast my eyes across the full six mile width of the lough over to Carrickfergus where my journey started a month ago. Apart from two boats at anchor, and a few yachts from the Royal North of Ireland Club moored out in the lough, there is not another vessel in sight. The 'busiest shipping lanes in Ireland' are empty. A collision with another boat would be impossible. Nothing else is moving – anywhere. The bustle of mercantile activity is certainly not apparent. Maybe it's early closing day.

As we enter the Victoria Channel, Belfast docks lie ahead and the yellow cranes of Harland and Wolff shipyard come into view. On either side we pass an unsightly sprawl of silent wharfs, quays, factories, container sheds, flour mills, power stations, dry docks and coal merchants. White, yellow and grey smoke pours from chimneys. We pass the Hong Kong registered *Quentin*. Crews from the *Olemar* and *Robin* from Limassol give us a wave as we pass.

We approach the red brick structure of Harland and Wolff and come to the point where the Victoria Channel meets the River Lagan. Past Queen's

Island wharf we turn into the small, almost hidden, Clarendon Dock where I disembark and salute Brian.

It's five o'clock when I arrive in a rain-sodden Belfast. Rush hour traffic is busy around Corporation Street. I walk past a tall office block and through the front gate of the harbour offices on to the road. The rain is turning into hailstones so I shelter in the Lifeboat Bar and watch buses, taxis and cars sitting bumper to bumper. I refuse the temptation to take public transport. When the rain ends I walk out into the fresh sunshine and complete the mile and a half journey home on foot over the Albert Bridge and along the Ravenhill Road.

POSTSCRIPT

Thumbs up for Ireland

It had been a struggle to get around the country; a long cold wet hard struggle. From day one I knew it would never be easy. It was not a task I'd undertaken lightly.

Hitchhikers are totally reliant on the whim of charity and the good nature of passing motorists. But since my early days of hitching in the seventies I think it has become more difficult. There's not the same willingness on the part of drivers, especially women, to stop. The thrill of the open road is still there though. And it remains a world of pure chance. For nearly four weeks the ordinary rules of life did not apply and I felt a little melancholy at the end of twenty-seven days on the road spent in the company of strangers. With the smells of the sea as a continual presence, and the rain a constant companion, I had watched spring passing imperceptibly into summer (or was it winter?) and felt the silent rhythms of nature.

To a large degree I had fulfilled my initial goal and in a small measure had followed my dream. I'd satisfied a desire and a longing to see the country and meet the people. I was forced to explain my life history, job details, views on politics, unions, the weather, football, the environment, and the state of the economy, north and south, to the many different people from whom I'd bummed lifts. I'd met farmers, fishermen, sailors, yachtsmen and women, lock-pilots, delivery men, teachers, trade unionists, technicians, mechanics, panel beaters, architects, businessmen, salesmen, singers, retired couples, mountaineers, restaurateurs, archaeologists, ornithologists and a never-ending stream of German tourists.

I'd passed through several hundred towns, villages and hamlets, negotiated countless roundabouts, ate numerous dull meals, slept in twenty-six different beds, and witnessed blood-red sunsets and dazzling seascapes. I had tasted solitude and made friendships.

For the first time ever in my life I became a dog-lover. The car-chasers, the hair-shedders, the rubbish-collectors, the rucksack-nibblers, the doggy-paddlers, the lamp-post lovers, the training shoe-fetishists, the tail-waggers, the limping-labradors and the stray collies were my bosom pals who shared the long hours spent by the side of quiet roads. To my total surprise I found them friendly and unaggressive.

My trip was also a journey of exploration in which I discovered the twelve Apostles, the eleven flowers of Dunluce, the ten townlands of Omeath, the nine daughters' blowhole, the eight wide-eyed children of Bundoran, the seven sisters of County Antrim, the six fruit juices of Ardeelan, the Fivemilebridge ox-eye daisies, the Four Alls and three fingers of west Cork, the two faces of Cobh Cathedral and a Wicklow man in a pear tree.

It was Ireland beside the sea at first hand. A country still indelibly wedded to the sea, and at least on the west coast, a green country unsullied by motorways. A land with a people obsessed by winning money in a weekly lottery and by teenagers who spend their evenings dancing to an empty orchestra.

A country where you get the impression that each town is competing to outdo the other twenty miles away or across the lough by building a bigger and more lavish marina, heritage base or interpretative centre. Centres that are being built with speed and greed, simply because money from Europe is available and because there is a deadline on the spending of those funds. I think it's safe to say that if the present splurge continues then in another few years there will be more interpretative centres than fastfood carry outs. Yet the centres are certain to play an increasingly important role into the next century as Ireland tries to capture more of the tourism market. (In fact, as you read these words, the sods on some of them will already have been turned and building work begun).

Then there are the seaside resorts which have a feeling of incompleteness about them unless they contain gargantuan man-made weather proof concrete sheds or artificial theme parks. Generally speaking I found them unattractive towns, catering for families, but seemingly unconcerned about their appearance.

In my head are imprints of the boring architectural similarity on the edge of towns: the petrol station and supermarket, the caravan site, the rows of small terraces and modern bungalows. I'd managed to avoid city centres with their identikit shops but found the pattern of town life was repeated throughout the journey. Many once entrancing towns have become bloated with ugly housing developments and ranch style bungalows. On the positive side though they have escaped the worst effects of twentieth century development. They are refreshingly free of shopping centres and, in most cases, have retained their original shop fronts.

The coastline has changed and is changing considerably. The Irish Sea, as well as being overfished, is radioactive and polluted. It has become a dustbin for industrial and toxic waste. On the west coast scientists believe that erosion of some areas will continue with rising sea levels and westerly storms. It's also believed beaches and dunes will move and break up. But despite all this there are miles of clear unpolluted beaches and images in my mind of an infinitely changing landscape. The over-riding and lasting impression is of a people who offered me nothing but kindness, hospitality, politeness and generosity.

It is a land with a vivid past. Each village has its own story to tell with its own characters. History, archaeology and botany surround the traveller who is willing to search it out. And, without wanting to sound like a blurb from one of the tourist board guides that I'd been reading, Ireland is a rewarding country full of myth, anecdote and superstition. My only regret is that I did not have more time to stay longer in each place.

When I reach home, as if to reassure myself that I have completed the circuit, I look at the map and go through a random incantation of names: Youghal, Killala, Dunmore East, Ballydehob, Killybegs, Sneem, Carlingford, Bastardstown, Ballybunion . . . the names trail away and I fold the map. I sit down with a large sigh, a large glass of port, and put up my feet. I am travel weary and talked out. I'm suffering information overload. All I want to do for the next few days is stare into space or at the ceiling and talk to no-one. As far as I'm concerned it can rain from now until doomsday. Physically I also feel weak. My shoulders ache from carrying the ruck; my legs and arms have a heavy feel; my feet have collected blisters and my toes are sitting at odd angles. I take a long look at what made it all possible – the curves of my thumbs and the POSSLQ. Glad to be home again, because *Hic Habitat Felicitas* – Here Lives Happiness.

APPENDIX I

Chronology of the journey

DAY	DATE (1991)	FROM	TO	DISTANCE in miles total
1	May 31st	Belfast	Ballycastle	70
2	June 1st	Ballycastle	Castlerock	35 (105)
3	June 2nd	Castlerock	Dunfanaghy	90 (195)
4	June 3rd	Dunfanaghy	Burtonport	34 (229)
5	June 4th	Burtonport	Rossnowlagh	69 (298)
6	June 5th	Rossnowlagh	Killala	100 (398)
7	June 6th	Killala	Belmullet	45 (443)
8	June 7th	Belmullet	Westport Quay	49 (492)
9	June 8th	Westport Quay	Clifden	46 (538)
10	June 9th	Clifden	Aran Islands	65 (603)
11	June 10th	Oatquarter	Kinvarra	22 (625)
12	June 11th	Kinvarra	Lahinch	37 (662)
13	June 12th	Lahinch	Ballybunion	52 (714)
14	June 13th	Ballybunion	Dingle	55 (769)
15	June 14th	Dingle	Glenbeigh	38 (807)
16	June 15th	Glenbeigh	Castletownbere	109 (916)
17	June 16th	Castletownbere	Schull	55 (971)
18	June 17th	Schull	Scilly	50 (1,021)
19	June 18th	Scilly	Youghal	43 (1,064)
20	June 19th	Youghal	Dunmore East	55 (1,119)
21	June 20th	Dunmore East	Kilmore Quay	32 (1,151)
22	June 21st	Kilmore Quay	Courtown	40 (1,191)
23	June 22nd	Courtown	Greystones	42 (1,233)
24	June 23rd	Greystones	Howth	25 (1,258)
25	June 24th	Howth	Carlingford	83 (1,341)
26	June 25th	Carlingford	Portaferry	50 (1,391)
27	June 26th	Portaferry	Belfast	45 (1,436)

APPENDIX II   List of botanical species

Alexanders	*Smyrnium olusatrum*
Bird's foot trefoil	*Lotus corniculatus*
Black medick	*Medicago lupulina*
Bogbean	*Menyanthes trifoliata*
Bog cotton	*Eriophorum angustifolium*
Bog mint	*Mentha aquatica*
Bulbous buttercup	*Ranunculus bulbosus*
Burnet rose	*Rosa pimpinellifolia*
Common buttercup	*Ranunculus acris*
Common butterwort	*Pinguicula vulgaris*
Corn poppy	*Papaver rhoeas*
Cuckoo flower	*Cardamine pratensis*
Dog rose	*Rosa canina*
Early purple orchid	*Orchis mascula*
Escallonia	*Escallonia rubra*
Foxglove	*Digitalis purpurea*
Fuchsia	*Fuchsia magellanica*
Hare's foot clover	*Trifolium arvense*
Hawthorn	*Crataegus monogyna*
Heartsease	*Viola arvensis*
Irish spurge	*Euphorbia hiberna*
Kidney vetch	*Anthyllis vulneraria*
Lousewort	*Pedicularis sylvatica*
Marsh marigold	*Caltha palustris*
Meadow cranesbill	*Geranium pratense*
Milkwort	*Polygala vulgaris*
Ox-eye daisy	*Chrysanthemum leucanthemum*
Ragged robin	*Lychnis flos-cuculi*
Red valerian	*Centranthus ruber*
Rhododendron	*Rhododendron ponticum*
Sea campion	*Silene maritima*
Sea holly	*Eryngium maritimum*
Seaside centaury	*Erythraea centaurium*
Sea thrift	*Armeria maritima*
Shrubby cinquefoil	*Potentilla fruticosa*
Spotted orchid	*Dactylorhiza fuchsii*
Sundew	*Drosera rotundifolia*
Wild thyme	*Thymus praecox*
Yellow flag	*Iris pseudacorus*
Yellow rattle	*Rhinanthus minor*

APPENDIX III

Acronyms used in the book

POSSLQ	Person of Opposite Sex Sharing Living Quarters
UKOGBANI	United Kingdom Of Great Britain And Northern Ireland
DOIM	Dear Old Irish Mother
CIE	Cram In Everybody
NIMBY	Not In My Back Yard
SAGA	Send All Grannies Away
DINKIES	Double Income No Kids
JOLLIES	Jet-setting Oldies with Lots of Lolly
YAKS	Young, Adventurous, Keen and Single
SINBAD	Single Income, No Boyfriend And Desperate
DART	Delays Are Really Trendy
DUMBOS	Drunken, Upperclass, Middle-aged Businessmen Over the limit

APPENDIX IV

The Amstrad PCW 9512, on which this book was typed, has a mind all of its own. Had it chosen to use the suggested replacement names from its automatic dictionary for the counties, towns and villages through which I passed, the result would have been a map unrecognized by cartographers the length and breadth of the country.

Carrickfergus – Carboniferous
Cushendun – Cushiness
Ballycastle – Babysat
Portrush – Porous
Castlerock – Candlewick
Donegal – Doleful
Burtonport – Butterwort
Bundoran – Buckbean
Sligo – Slag
Belmullet – Beguiled
Ballyconneely – Ballistically
Kilrush – Kibosh
Ballybunion – Babylonian
Dingle – Dibble
Cahersiveen – Caesarean
Castlecove – Casserole
Sneem – Sneer
Castletownbere – Candlepower
Bantry – Bakery
Crookhaven – Crocheted
Ballydehob – Ballyhoo
Castletownsend – Categorized
Skibbereen – Skippered
Youghal – Yoga
Wexford – Webfoot
Gorey – Gooey
Greystones – Gravestones
Malahide – Malaise
Portmarnock – Portmanteau
Louth – Loath
Castlebellingham – Cartwheeling
Portaferry – Poriferal

SELECT BIBLIOGRAPHY

There is an infinite choice of books, maps and guides about Ireland. Here are a few I used, quoted from, or otherwise enjoyed reading or browsing through in the writing of this book.

AA Road Book of Ireland. Belfast, Automobile Association, 1962.
Atlas of Ireland. Royal Irish Academy, Dublin, 1979.
County Wexford Civil Survey, 1654. Irish Manuscripts Commission.
Crosbie Jane E.M. *A Tour of The Ardes 1910-35*, Friar's Bush Press, *Belfast,* 1990.
D'Arcy, Gordon. *Pocket Guide to the Birds of Ireland*, Appletree Press, Belfast, 1986.
Griffith Valuation, Griffith Richard, *1853*.
Hutchinson, Clive D. *Birds in Ireland*, T. & A. D. Poyser for the Irish Wildbird Conservancy, Calton, Staffordshire, 1989.
Hore's Wexford, Ed. by Philip Herbert Hore, Elliot Stock, London, 1901.
Lynam, Joss. *Irish Peaks*, Constable & Co Ltd, London, 1982.
MacGill, Patrick. *The Navvy Poet*, The Collected Poetry of Patrick MacGill, Caliban Books, London, 1984.
Mason, Thomas H. *The Islands of Ireland*, B.T. Batsford Ltd, London, 1936.
Morton, H.V. *In Search of Ireland*, Methuen & Co. Ltd, London, 1930.
O'Connell, James. *The Meaning of Irish Place Names*, Blackstaff Press, Belfast, 1979.
Official Guide to Co. Wexford, Wexford Chamber of Commerce, 1963.
Official Guide to Killarney, Irish Tourist Association, Dublin, 1934.
Penguin Book of Contemporary Irish Poetry, Penguin, London, 1990.
Pigot's Directory and Guide to Ireland, J. Pigot & Co, London, 1824.
Praeger, Robert Lloyd. *The Way That I Went*, Second edition, Hodges, Figgis & Co, and London, Methuen & Co Ltd, Dublin, 1939.
Praeger, Robert Lloyd. *Natural History of Ireland*: A sketch of its flora and fauna, Collins, London, 1950.
Robinson, Tim. *Stones of Aran*, Part 1: Pilgrimage, Penguin-Viking, London and Lilliput Press, Dublin, 1986.
Robinson, Tim. *Connemara. Bilingual route map and gazetteer*, Roundstone, Folding Landscapes, 1990.
Ross, Ruth Isabel. *Pocket Guide to Irish Wild Flowers*, Appletree Press, Belfast, 1987.
Rowan, Alistair. *The Buildings of Ireland: North-West Ulster*, Advisory Editor: Nikolaus Pevsner, Penguin, London, 1979.

Thackeray, William. *The Irish Sketch Book*, 1842. New edition, Blackstaff Press, Belfast, 1985.

Theroux, Paul. *The Kingdom by the Sea*, Hamish Hamilton, London, 1983.

Webb, D.A. *An Irish Flora*, Dundalgan Press, Dundalk, 1943.

Some other books, not related to Ireland, mentioned in the text.

Ayres, Alex. *Greatly Exaggerated: The wit and wisdom of Mark Twain*, Barrie & Jenkins, London, 1988.

Morris, Jan. *Travels*, Faber and Faber, London, 1976.

Steinbeck, John. *Travels With Charley*, Heinemann, London, 1962.

Twain, Mark. *The Adventures of Tom Sawyer*, 1876. New edition, Penguin Books, London, 1986.

Welsh, Ken. *Hitchhiker's Guide to Europe*. Twelfth edition, Fontana/Collins, London, 1991.